# BEING BIRACIAL

## where our secret worlds collide

sarah ratliff + bryony sutherland

Being Biracial: Where Our Secret Worlds Collide

Coquí Press
41 Avenida Fernando Luis Ribas
#449
Utuado, Puerto Rico 00641
http://coquipress.com

ISBN 10: 1937660664
ISBN 13: 978-1-937660-66-6
eBook ISBN: 978-1-937660-71-0


First edition: September 2015
Second edition: January 2016
Third edition: May 2017

Printed in the USA

# REVIEWS OF BEING BIRACIAL:
## where our secret worlds collide

*Being Biracial: Where Our Secret Worlds Collide* is the best of both worlds. It is not only academic, nor is it only commercial. Sarah Ratliff and Bryony Sutherland have indeed found a way to take a subject that will appeal to everyone, from interracial families, to the multiracial population, to non-fiction readers, and to academics. It is a book that needs to be read by anyone interested in diversity and the multiracial viewpoint.
*Susan Graham, President, Project RACE, Inc.*

A must read for the family members and friends of those who identify as Biracial, especially those readers who come from a dominant racial category.
*Alec MacLeod, MFA, Professor, Interdisciplinary Studies, California Institute of Integral Studies*

A heart and soul-baring endeavor; *Being Biracial* reminds us that beneath the sheaths that cover our skin and bones, beat hearts that long for love and acceptance.
*Edie Weinstein, MSW, LSW, host of the VividLife radio show, It's All About Relationships*

*Being Biracial* pulls back the curtain and shows in interesting, stirring, and captivating ways what the life of those who are multiracial is like, which cannot help but raise the level of empathy and understanding of all.
*Alex Barnett (White and Jewish, father to a Biracial son), host of the Multiracial Family Man podcast*

This is an engaging read as well as an educational treasure. Buy it, read it and enjoy it. If you teach contemporary sociology or diversity, add it to your curriculum immediately.
*Stephanie Bader, MBA, Adjunct Faculty at Pima Community College*

*Being Biracial* depicts our multidimensional world, in both its unifying and divisive aspects, and ultimately leaves the reader with a sense of belonging that transcends skin color.
*Shannon Luders-Manuel, MA (White and Black), critical mixed race scholar and writer*

It is not easy to navigate through two or more worlds, and oftentimes very frustrating as people of Biracial descent are criticized by many and accepted by few. Very honest and at times painful, these stories are a true reflection of what is obvious but not talked about in our society. The fact that Biracial individuals make up one of the fastest growing populations makes this book so important.
*John Reed Ph.D., Author: It's Not Always Black And White: Caught Between Two Worlds*

*Being Biracial* is brutally honest, heart-wrenchingly frank and unapologetic in its commentary. Through narratives of experiences, authors of various racial make-ups and ethnicities describe how people go about the business of treating others who appear to be "uncategorizable" by race.
*Cynthia Sass, JD (Black, with a Biracial family)*

What was amazing about *Being Biracial* was how familiar it was: the pain of not being accepted by either group, having to choose sides, feeling the need to justify one's existence. The stories show brutal honesty, pain, redemption and even the kindness to forgive those who show prejudice toward them.
*Denise Lynch (White and Hispanic)*

*Being Biracial* will make people think. It will also pave the way for important and enlightening conversations that might not otherwise take place.
*Deb Kingsbury (White with North African heritage)*

*Being Biracial* is a book for all people, regardless of ethnicity. Some day perhaps we will celebrate our differences and our commonalities without judgment. This book will help us get there.
*Joan Kirchheimer (White, mother of two Biracial children)*

# DEDICATION

*For Emily Orick, who despite being a successful writer for* The
Atlantic *and* The New Yorker *magazines, was never able to realize
her dream of publishing a novel.*
*This book is for you, Mom.*
*Love, Sarah*

# CONTENTS

# INTRODUCTION

## Bryony's Story

Sarah and I met online. Before you assume that we were part of some "lonely hearts" brigade, it wasn't anything quite like that. We both work in what might be described as the ultra-modern arena of online freelancing. As writers and editors, we work almost exclusively on the Internet, producing and refining content for websites, companies and individuals hailing from all around the globe. We rarely—if ever—meet our clients in person. The platform we used when we met was a leading freelancing source, and we ranked highly within the Writing & Translation category. In fact, Sarah's business had long been the top listed company. Frankly put, I was more than a little intimidated by her.

When we did eventually connect through an independent initiative, the sparks of friendship flew thick and fast. It was bewildering. Other than our careers, how could I possibly have so much in common with this exotic (sorry, Sarah, I know you hate that word) goat farmer living on the other side of the planet—on a tropical Caribbean island, no less? Yet I did. From musical idols to religious observations, from feminism and vegetarianism to taste in cheese and love of the original *Star Trek* series, we connected. All via the magic of email—the modern equivalent of being pen pals.

Then one day we were comparing articles we had written and I directed her to one of mine, published on a women's health and beauty site. Sarah's praise for the feature came back swiftly, but there was something else. She informed me in the politest way possible that the site was disregarding half of its potential audience by only featuring White women in the illustrations. I was amazed. Having nothing to do with the visual aspect of this site—and rarely even looking at it as my responsibilities ended with the content—I investigated. Sarah was right. This women's site was far too pink for its own good.

Sarah had written to me, in her words, "as a woman of colour." She was painfully keen for me, a White woman, not to take offence. I don't think Sarah expected my response. The thing is, I'm what I thought of back then as "colour blind." My husband's Black and our children are mixed race. Many of our friends and their families are similarly mixed up. I realised with a jolt that I'm so used to seeing multi-coloured faces before me, that I didn't even register race anymore. And that is where Sarah and I differed.

When I looked at photos of Sarah, I thought she was of Hispanic descent. In fact, she could easily have been mistaken for White. I hadn't given this a moment's thought. Yet now she was telling me that, despite being only a quarter African American, she identified Black, and this was a big part of her life. This was fascinating to me. If she felt this way now, how would my children and their children identify in the years to come?

As we discussed our Biracial families, the conversation spiralled off in a whole new direction, which ultimately led to this book, a deeper friendship and a change in the way I'll view this topic forever. And that is where I'll let Sarah pick up the story.

## Sarah's Story

Race is a topic I think about constantly. I have to assume it's because I was raised by parents who, because of their racial and ethnic differences, didn't shy away from subjects many families have the luxury of glossing over.

Although I go into more detail in my essay, I am Caucasian, African American and Japanese. My father's father was born and raised in Germany. My paternal grandmother was Dutch and Irish. My maternal grandmother was Black and she—like most African Americans—was a descendent of slaves from West Africa. Because birth, marriage and death records for slaves were unimportant for slaves' masters/owners to keep, I am unable to trace that side of my mother's family beyond the early 1800s. However, I am certain from the oral history handed down that only a few generations back, my ancestors were slaves living in the Deep South. My maternal grandfather was Japanese and he came to the United States in 1918.

This, of course, made my mother Biracial.

As my brothers and I grew up, our parents ensured we saw things from every angle. So much so that now, as an adult, when a discussion gets going, I am incapable of taking a myopic view and of keeping my thoughts to myself.

Bryony's version of how we became friends is completely accurate—right down to me poking my nose into her business and letting her know that the site where she has a byline was lacking women of color in the accompanying photos. This is something that irks me about the Internet and popular culture, to be perfectly honest. It's something I notice immediately and, if I land on a website where there is an obvious absence of color, I leave. I won't even bother considering buying that product or service.

So why did I bother to say anything to Bryony? Because I had gotten to know her and figured she was well worth giving the benefit of the doubt. Aside from that, the article that got me to sit up and take notice was one in which she was covering the double standard of people working themselves up in a tizzy over a woman breastfeeding in public. I made the assumption that if Bryony were an advocate of women's rights, she could—at the very minimum—be open to the idea of advocating for folks of different ethnicities.

Surprised was I to learn that Bryony was not only open, but that she was married to a Black man.

I have always wanted to write a book about being Biracial. I have a lot to say on the topic (as you'll see when you read my essay, which is far and away the longest). Realizing Bryony was serious about collaborating with me on this book put the fire under my butt I needed. Although we could have written it entirely ourselves, we agreed that allowing others to tell their stories drives the point home better. As outspoken and opinionated as I am (and I am learning Bryony to be), I don't think people want to hear from just us.

Truth be told, we haven't really guided this project much. We put it out there when we started looking for contributors and the book took on a life of its own. All we really knew was that we wanted essays from contributors from around the world, but as pitches from authors came in, we knew we were on to something. I'll explain. I have personalized my racial identity for forty-eight years. Of course I have; it's my life and that's pretty normal. However, getting out of my own head so I could absorb other people's stories has been enlightening, sobering and affirming.

I know what my experiences have been, which have certainly shaped the woman I have become, but if this journey has taught me anything, it's that we are all dichotomous: we are fragile and yet amazingly strong. Susceptible and sensitive to what others think, say and feel about us and the actions they take against us, our experiences make us stronger, more resilient and after a point, impervious and more resolute in our missions.

Because of my experiences, which have informed my racial identity, I had become hardened and pessimistic. My husband and I moved to Puerto Rico in part to escape the racism going on in the United States, but because

I am very active politically and socially, I couldn't stop myself from looking at the news "up there." One needn't look far to get hopping mad (I cite several examples in my own essay), and I am very expressive, as anyone who knows me can attest to.

Sometimes, along with expressing anger, I communicate my pessimism.

And then along came Bryony with her "Life is beautiful. I couldn't be happier. I am truly blissful." And I began to think, *What's this woman on? I want some of that...*I made this assumption Bryony was living in a land of butterflies and rainbows. I saw her as this woman and one-half of a marriage who never faced adversity. These are obviously my hang-ups and they're not based in anything but me comparing my insides to her outsides. Theirs is a very functional family—indeed this is true. However, in working with Bryony this last year, I have come to see her as more complex and of course, both fragile and amazingly strong.

Both through reading the essays of all of our contributors and through my friendship with Bryony, I have started to soften a bit.

## Our Secret Worlds

Biracial people are multi-faceted people. We are all people. Yet few can resist the urge to throw in their two cents about race, which reminds us of watching Mr. Spock—arguably the world's most memorable Biracial character—in the original *Star Trek* series, playing a game of multi-level chess. Interestingly, as Biracial people continue trending, the conversation is beginning to change.

Nowadays, being Biracial is as modern as our online relationship. At one time the focus was on race itself and the dynamics of belonging to one race or the other—wherever we humans lived. Today it's different. As more people see love as something that can transcend all else—including the comfort zone of "staying with one's own kind"—being Biracial will no longer be the anomaly, but rather the norm.

However, before we get there, we should probably define race. Some might say it's the color of one's skin and his or her features. Sarah would reject this as the sole descriptor, because if that were the case, she would be either White or Hispanic and have no Black or Japanese in her. Others say it's how we're raised, in which case, Bryony knows she has her work cut out for her. Yet others argue that race is merely a social construct designed to segregate people into the "Us" and "Them" camps. They have a point.

While we would love nothing more than to see us all as a unified race— by which we mean the "human" race, as so many "color blind" people put it—we aren't there yet and we doubt we will be in our lifetimes. And much as we hate racism, to pretend the obvious differences between us don't exist is a case of ignoring what is before our very eyes. So until then, race—with its multi-faceted layers—is a topic we'll be discussing for a long time. And as we continue mixing things up, being Biracial will no longer be something to fear, but rather something to embrace and be proud of.

Our journey writing this book has been illuminating, to say the least. Please note that we purposely sought to retain our authors' style in terms of U.S. vs UK spelling, and you may notice a few syntactical differences too. We hope the stories you're about to read will change your perspectives and open your eyes and hearts as they have ours.

Sarah Ratliff + Bryony Sutherland
September 2015

# CRIMINAL MISTAKES

## Sarah Ratliff—Puerto Rico

African American, Japanese, English, French,

Scandinavian, German, Dutch, and Irish

"For the fucking love of God, Emily! Why didn't you tell me you were *Black?*" Red in the face and on the verge of tears, the man posing the question wasn't sure whether to be sad, angry or confused.

He stared at the caramel-complected woman with the hint of Asian eyes on the other side of the door to his Manhattan apartment. She was as beautiful in person as he'd often imagined her to be. However, in his mind she had blue eyes and blonde hair. Sometimes her hair and eyes were brown and sometimes she had red hair, but her complexion was always *white* like his.

He started shaking his head.

She worked for a company owned and managed by White people. She held a position not often given to a woman, let alone a Black woman. "This just can't be," he mumbled to himself and motioned for her to come into his apartment.

Once inside, he took her raincoat, hat and gloves and hung them up in the closet. He looked more closely at her. She was stunning in her pale green dress and cream-colored, sling-back pumps. Tall—maybe five feet seven—slender, with high cheekbones and very feminine, he was almost embarrassed he found her so beautiful.

He led her to the living room. They sat down on the sofa next to each other. He offered her a glass of water.

She shook her head, no. The tears started coming. She avoided looking at him one moment, and the next all she could do was stare deeply at him. "George, I tried to...a few times. You said you didn't care." Now it was her turn to be sad, angry and confused.

"Did you really try or did you give up when I said that nothing you could say could change how I feel about you?" Was he conceding or did he want to make her accept the blame and even feel guilty for the impossible situation they found themselves in?

"Probably...maybe...possibly. I don't know, George. But, I did try, you remember. Maybe I should have pushed harder than just telling you there are things you should know about me. But you did say nothing could change how you feel about me. Is that still true?"

"Yes...it's true. I just don't know how to tell my parents. This isn't going to go over well, I am sure of that. There are things you need to know about my father.

"My father has always been a racist; comments he made about the few Black people in our town when I was growing up told me everything I needed to know. Growing up I assumed he just didn't like them. Something happened when I was seventeen years old that made it clear that he didn't just dislike them, but that he wished they would all...*die*, preferably violently.

"I saw a Black boy struggling in a lake by our house. I could see him through the fence. He was no more than a few hundred feet away. All I

8

would have needed to do is climb over the fence and I could have saved him from drowning. I saw him go down once, and I knew he couldn't swim. I started to untie my shoes so I could save him.

"My father pinned me from behind against the fence and he made me watch that poor kid drown. He told me, 'No nigger life is worth saving.'" George paused and looked up to the ceiling to hide the fact that he was starting to cry. He had never told anyone about this incident and he still carried the guilt with him for eighteen years that he allowed a person to die and he couldn't do anything about it.

Emily put her hand on his cheek.

"Emily," he said, composing himself, "my father grew up in Germany and he was genuinely happy all those Jews, Gypsies and homosexuals died in the Holocaust. He feels Hitler did society a favor by getting rid of—as he calls them—the filth. He is very outspoken about how much he hates anyone who isn't White and Catholic." He sighed. "This isn't going to end well. I am going to have to make a choice between you and my family. I know that's what's going to happen."

Emily knew what had to happen. She had been here before. Her first husband tried to make it work, but in the end, his family put too much pressure on him. He couldn't stand the pressure, and after only two years of marriage, Eugene asked for a divorce. It caught Emily by surprise because she had thought his parents were finally starting to come around.

She couldn't go through this again. She couldn't put anyone through this again. But the bigger question was, how did this happen again? How did she let this happen again?

"No, I refuse to allow you to do that. I will just...go. I can't let you make such a drastic decision—not for me!" Emily looked him straight in the eye. She held his hand, stood up and kissed him. He returned the kiss and let her hand go. "Goodbye, George. I will always love you. Society isn't ready for an interracial couple to be happy."

And with that, she was out of his life.

## The Racial and Political Climate in the 1950s

My parents met in 1958. At the time my father, George Orick, was working as the agent and manager for photographer W. Eugene Smith[1] while my mother, née Emily Allen, was a photojournalist for Magnum Photos[2], which represented Smith's work.

Assigned to interview Smith for an upcoming article, Emily was in constant phone contact with George. Over time, the calls became less about Smith and more about each other. They shared their pasts and their dreams, and it was clear they had a lot in common.

Both were products of the Great Depression. My father was born in 1923 and my mother was born in 1933. My father grew up in Schenectady, New York.

He had one brother. Their mother was able to retain her job as a schoolteacher while his father never really worked.

He was drafted at the age of nineteen to fight in World War II. He was honorably discharged after the war was over, and he used the GI Bill to go to Union College, also in Schenectady, to study journalism. He worked first for the *Schenectady Gazette* and then the *New York Times*. While at the *Times,* he met Smith (who at the time was working with *Life* magazine) and agreed to represent him.

My mother grew up in White Plains, New York (a suburb outside of New York City). Her father died when she was just five years old of pancreatic

---

[1] W. Eugene Smith: http://en.wikipedia.org/wiki/W._Eugene_Smith

[2] Magnum Photos: http://www.magnumphotos.com

cancer. My grandmother worked as a domestic for a well-off White family. She cooked, cleaned and managed the home. She worked for this family from the time she was in her early twenties until she died when she was seventy-one.

Not able to get a college education, my grandmother insisted my mother get excellent grades and go to a good college. Not having the money to pay for expensive tuition, a scholarship would be the only way my mother could achieve this.

My mother was eager to excel in school. She had all As in every subject except for math. By the time she was fourteen, because my mother was known to double up on classes, she was a senior in high school. The only class she had left was a history class.

Not wanting to be bored all day at school when she wasn't in history class, my mother decided to take Latin and German. She was already fluent in French.

When she took her college boards (today known as the SATs), she scored an extremely impressive 1570 out of 1600. The test consisted of two parts: English and Math. My mother's English score was perfect and her Math wasn't.

My mother applied for and was accepted to all of the Seven Sisters schools[3]. She decided to attend Barnard and study English, from which she'd hoped to get a job as a journalist. My mother got a full ride—not even needing to pay for books or her dorm room.

Securing a job straight out of college as a secretary for Magnum Photos, Emily then worked her way up to editor and eventually to photojournalist.

Both loved writing. My father was an extreme extrovert (no doubt this is where I get it from), and he got a thrill being in the thick of things,

---

[3] Seven Sisters colleges: http://en.wikipedia.org/wiki/Seven_Sisters_(colleges)

reporting about anything. Although it might have seemed odd to leave the *Times* to work for W. Eugene Smith, it wasn't really.

Smith was known for his realism, for telling the story exactly as it was. He was an advocate of women and people of color, and this resonated deeply with my father—who couldn't have been any more different from his father if he'd tried.

Although my mother had a love for words, the part she could have lived just as long without were the interviews and the interaction in general with people. She was an introvert's introvert.

My father cursed a lot and my mother never cursed, but their views were the same—even if they had different forms of expressing their opinions about them.

One day during one of their many phone calls, my father told my mother a secret he had been hiding from her.

"Emily, I am married."

She was crushed. "George, really? Why did you wait so long to tell me?"

"Well, because I had already been considering asking her for a divorce before I met you. I didn't want you to be the reason I left her. I wanted to be sure I was leaving for the right reasons." He paused. "Does that make sense?"

"So you were already having problems before we started talking?"

"Yes. Don't get me wrong. It's not her. There's nothing wrong with her. She's a very nice person. We were high school sweethearts, and when I was drafted to fight in the war, she promised to wait for me. I didn't believe she would, but she did. How could I not marry her? Nobody had ever been that loyal to me."

"So you married her more out of obligation than love?"

"Yes, that's fair to say. I don't think I ever really loved her in the grown up sense. We're very different. She is a product of her—and even my own—

upbringing. Her views haven't evolved much since high school. She's intelligent—well I doubt she's nearly as intelligent as you are—but she doesn't express opinions on anything. She won't take a stance on anything. She's very well meaning. I mean, everyone loves her. She is sweet and she will do anything for anyone, but I am sorry to say this, I am bored. There are only so many bridge games we can play—while not talking about anything of any substance—and Martinis I can drink before I start to wonder, 'Is there more to life than this?'"

"How long have you been deciding whether to leave?"

"About eight months. We had agreed that I would move to New York City and make a go of this job, but also consider whether there was a future for us."

"And?" My mother was known for never revealing what she was thinking or feeling.

"Even though I hated the idea of hurting her, filing for divorce was the best for both of us. When I met you, I knew I was making the best choice. The idea of meeting someone like you—smart, opinionated, informed and nice—I knew there was someone out there who was right for me."

"So now what?"

"Let's meet. I want to see you in person. We've been talking for months. Don't you think it's time?"

"Yes," my mother said, "but, George, there's something you need to know about me before you meet me."

"Are you married, too?"

"No, I am divorced."

"Do you have kids?"

"No, we were only married two years and I wasn't ready." She didn't want to tell him the real reason they divorced...not just yet. "But that's not it. I really need to share this with you before you meet me."

"Shhhhhhh! There's nothing you can tell me that would make me feel differently about you. Emily, I am falling in love with you." With that he hung up.

Then the shit hit the fan!

# Fighting for Equal Rights

*With the Civil Rights Movement (1954-1968) well underway in the United States, relations between African Americans and Whites were tense—which is, of course putting things mildly.*

*The modern Civil Rights Movement began as a quiet, dignified and principled response to everyday manifestations of oppression. The Montgomery Bus Boycott of 1955-56 heralded a new era in the fight for fairness and equality in the Jim Crow South, and ultimately inspired African Americans of all ages and backgrounds to assert their rights and privileges through any means necessary.*

*This notable event—and the amazing transformation in expectations it wrought—were not followed immediately by further bold action, but with grassroots organizing and reflective debates over the direction and future of this action-oriented rejection of the status quo.*

*The sit-in campaigns that tackled segregation in public facilities would not begin in earnest for another five years, but following the Montgomery Bus Boycott, everyone in the African American community—both North and South—realized a new day had arrived.*

*The commitment to non-violence and legal reform that defined the early Civil Rights Movement was a deliberate choice, one that even the most ambitious of reformers in 1950s America believed was necessary to bring lasting change and authentic achievement.*

*America's Cold War paranoia over the so-called Communist menace gave opponents of social change a convenient weapon to use against those* who dreamed of something better, and advocates for civil rights knew that in the present climate, campaigns for change couldn't challenge ideological pillars like patriotism, Christianity and an opposition to radicalism if they expected to succeed.

In the wake of the Montgomery Bus Boycott and the formation of the Southern Christian Leadership Council, the fight for better education took center stage in the struggle for civil rights below the Mason-Dixon line.

The Supreme Court's 1954 Brown v. the Board of Education *ruling that declared school segregation unconstitutional opened the doors of change, but making sure that decision was translated into actual practice in defiant ex-Confederate states was going to take a Herculean effort, as the situation in the Little Rock school system in 1957 proved so conclusively. Hatred dies but it dies hard, and no one had any illusions about the difficulties that lined the path to racial progress.*

*Meanwhile in the North, civil rights activists embraced a more comprehensive, multi-faceted approach in their coordinated attacks against the barriers of legalized discrimination. Mass migrations from the rural South to the urban North had altered the demographic characteristics of America's Black population forever, creating sizable enclaves of African Americans who could pool their talents, resources and desires in environments where the hair-trigger threat of violent retaliation was no longer present, except perhaps in encounters with the police.*

*With an expanded population base and rising expectations following the close of World War II (where more than a million African Americans served in support of the war effort in one form or another), African American community leaders in northern cities were in a greater position of strength as they pushed persistently and without compromise throughout the 1940s and 50s for an end to segregation in the school system, in housing, in public facilities, in the job market and eventually in marriage.*

*Despite the attention paid to the situation in the South, the very same obstacles to freedom limited the life possibilities of African Americans in the North, where racial prejudice was only slightly less rampant and pervasive. We have been taught to associate the term "Civil Rights Movement" almost exclusively with the actions of African Americans in the South, but the struggle for fairness and equality in the North actually preceded the more publicized Southern campaigns and, in general, reformers in the North focused on a wider variety of cultural, social, political and economic issues than their brethren in the former Confederate states.*

*In the South and nationally, the Civil Rights Movement eventually progressed beyond the gradualist, legalistic approach that defined its earliest stages, and it was the example set by Northern civil rights activists that helped light the way to a broader campaign for social justice. New York City, with the largest African American population in the country following the great southern migration, was a bastion of civil rights activism in the fifteen-year period from the end of World War II to the election of JFK in 1960, when the attack on Jim Crow laws and other forms of outrageous discrimination in the South finally took off in earnest.*

## As if Being Black Weren't Complicated Enough, You're Japanese Too?

I think it's fair to say that my father wasn't racist. I never once got a hint of this from him. However, having a father who was overtly racist toward everyone meant my father would have to make a choice. Choose his family, or choose love and the chance to be happy. The question was: was he prepared to?

Clearly he was, otherwise I wouldn't be here writing about them. I am alive, which means they got back together and confronted my father's father (I have never been able to refer to him as my grandfather).

Predictably, things did not go well.

A few days after the meeting in his apartment, my father showed up at my mother's job with flowers. The receptionist showed him to my mother's office.

My mother had been trying to concentrate long enough to write her article about W. Eugene Smith. All she could think of was the first and last time she met the man she had fallen in love with. She stared off into space and put her pen down. As she did, she heard a knock on the door.

When the door opened, she saw what she hadn't expected to see. Before the door closed, unashamed who could hear, my father said, "Emily, I love you. I am ready to face my father. If you'll have me, I would like to marry you."

The receptionist gave my mother the okay sign, grinned from ear-to-ear and closed the door behind my father.

My mother stood up. Not quite certain she was ready to believe him, instead of hugging him, she showed him the seat in front of her desk. My father sat down.

"What made you change your mind?" she asked, fighting the tears.

"I had a long talk with Smith." Having been in the Navy during World War II, my father often called people by their last names—of course, he was referring to W. Eugene Smith.

"What did he say?"

"He said this whole thing is fucked up. The world is going fucking crazy, but it won't always be this way. He thinks one day Blacks and Whites will be equal and what we're experiencing...it won't always be this way.

"I've checked. It's completely legal for us to get married in the state of New York. They've never had anti-miscegenation laws on the books." Things were looking up.

*He is serious,* she thought to herself. *He's willing to risk being disowned by his father...for me!*

"What about your wife?" Okay, fair question.

"I was going to file for divorce before I met you. I filed a few days ago. I am just waiting for it to be granted. As soon as it is, let's get married."

"What about your parents?" Another fair question.

"My mother will love you. My father won't let her love you and that will be that. He is a very controlling man. But here's the thing, Emily...if I don't do this, what do I have? I can live my life, sure, but without you in it...I don't have a life." He was serious.

"Well, I suppose I should probably tell you that I am not just Black. I am actually half Black and half Japanese. My father was from Osaka, Japan. He came to the U.S. in 1918. He met my mother in 1925 and they fell in love. Nobody in my town ever really accepted my father. It was bad enough we were Black—in fact, we were one of only two Black families in our town. We lived in almost total isolation. The KKK threw rocks through our windows pretty regularly. They burned one family's house down."

"Jesus, Emily! What the fuck is wrong with this country? Segregation of Black and White, throwing the Japanese in internment camps during World War II, and all the bloody wars with countries to gain power or control their natural resources. When does it fucking end? When can we just live in peace?"

"One day, George, it will. It won't be in our lifetime, though. But one day, everyone will be equal and nobody will have to ask these questions."

## Guess Who's Coming to Dinner?

By the end of 1958, my father got what he had been hoping to receive every day since he decided to marry my mother. New York State had granted him a divorce.

They wasted no time and decided to get the meeting from hell out of the way. That weekend they drove to Schenectady so he could introduce his parents to his fiancée. During the three-hour drive, they talked incessantly about what to expect.

My father was very clear. "If my father says anything racist, we will walk out and I promise never to see him again. But I have to give him the benefit of the doubt."

Predictably my father's father was, shall we say, less than hospitable to my mother. My grandmother welcomed them in and gave each a hug and a kiss. I never met her, as she died when I was two. There was major drama when my father went to the hospital to say goodbye to her. How she ended up with my father's father is beyond me!

My father's father looked at my mother and said, "So you divorced Barbara and found yourself a nigger to sponge off you?" Charming man, wasn't he?

"Dad, I wanted to introduce you to the woman I am going to marry. And no, she isn't a sponge. She is a photojournalist with the agency that represents Smith." *There,* he thought, *that'll change his mind about Black people.*

"Who did she fuck to get that job?"

My parents never even took off their coats. My father kissed my grandmother and told her he loved her, and he and my mother walked out the door. "Don't ever bring that nigger back into my house. As long as you're with her, you are no son of mine!"

I know it had to have killed my mother, but she never allowed my father's father the satisfaction of seeing that he'd rattled her. Instead, she held her head high as they left.

How can someone's hate be so strong? He didn't know my mother, so how could he just judge her like that?

19

This is, of course, the emotional me speaking. The other me, the more cynical me, the one who's been slapped around a few times by society's judgmental thinking, gets it. I don't want to get it, but I do.

And this mean bastard made good on his promise. A few weeks later my father got a call from his brother who told him their father had disowned him—until he came to his senses. Their father revised his will to reflect the change.

My parents' response was to start planning their wedding. Fortunately, reactions from my mother's camp were very different. My maternal grandmother immediately accepted my father as her son and gave them her blessing. All she wanted was for my mother to be happy. And she was happy—for the most part. How can one be completely happy knowing that society is against you for no other reason than the color of your skin?

## And So it Goes...

My parents were married on January 29, 1960 in a very small ceremony at City Hall in New York City. Afterward, they had a small gathering at the apartment my mother shared with her two roommates, Didi and Janet.

Realizing things weren't going to be easy for them as an interracial couple, they talked seriously about their options. New York was one of the more progressive northern states and New York City was probably the most progressive in the United States.

The southeastern U.S. was out of the question. With Jim Crow/anti-miscegenation laws preventing my mother from eating in the same establishments as my father, from sitting next to him on a bus, renting an apartment with him and, oh yeah, being legally married to him, this was not an option.

Although New York didn't pose any legal restrictions on interracial marriage (it was one of just six states where no laws were ever passed barring it), attitudes among normal everyday folk weren't very accepting.

My parents would go to restaurants and people quite literally gawked at them. Several times my parents told me about instances where the manager came over to ask, "Sir, might you and your dinner companion be more comfortable eating dinner elsewhere?"

My mother learned to keep her thoughts and feelings to herself. My father had an inability to not be reactionary—I am assuming this is where I get it from.

He often replied with the same words, "No, my wife and I are happy eating dinner here. If your asshole patrons want to leave, they can be my guest. We have a legal right to be here."

But at some point, it gets old defending one's right to eat a meal out in public and fight disapproval *en masse*. And within a couple of months, they decided to leave the racist United States with its backward laws and morals.

Unfortunately, I will never know what made them choose Nigeria. All I know is that one day they were on a plane headed for its capital, Lagos, to spend what they hoped would be the rest of their lives.

Saying goodbye to their friends was difficult. Unsurprisingly, my father's friends (most of whom were White and had only known privilege) fell into two camps:

- Hey, things will get better. Just stick it out!
- If things don't go well, I will happily introduce you to my cousin/sister/niece/next door neighbor.

Conversely, reactions from my mother's friends—who spanned the ethnic rainbow—were all over the place. They ranged from:

- Honey, is he really worth it?
- Couldn't you have picked a nice Negro man to fall in love with? (This came from a White friend.)
- I could never be as brave as you!
- I once had a crush on a White man and I knew he wouldn't have given me a second glance, and so I let it go.
- What will your children look like? Have you even thought about them?
- Why would you bring trouble on yourself like this?
- I am here for you, if you ever need a shoulder to cry on when he leaves you for a White woman.

And the last came from the one woman with whom my mother remained friends until the day my mother died:

"Em, I don't imagine your journey is going to be easy, but I support you no matter what. When others turn their backs on you or say snide remarks, I will be the one holding out my hand for you—always."

If my parents felt they were leaving nothing but problems and going to Utopia, they couldn't have done worse, actually. Months away from being granted independence from English colonization (which began in 1914), the country was about to go into serious upheaval.

Could my parents have known this? Maybe not about Nigeria specifically, but certainly that it was imminent because England was in the process of what it termed "the decolonization of Africa," meaning it was bound to happen sooner rather than later or never.

Now with Nigeria as the backdrop of their story, my parents attempted to live their lives—as would any other couple. My oldest brother Nicholas was born in 1963 when my mother was thirty years old. This was big news for my father, who'd tried unsuccessfully to have kids with his first wife. He'd begun to think there was something wrong with him.

At forty, he was considerably older than the fathers he and my mother had made friends with over the previous three years. My parents were able to forge some bonds with many people (Nigerians, Indians, Americans,  British, Australians and Canadians), despite whatever political turmoil was going on.

Benjamin was born in 1964, and I was born three days before Christmas in 1966. We all looked different. Friends of my parents used to joke they had one Black child (Nicholas), one Asian child (Benjamin) and one we're-not-sure-what-she's-going-to-be: maybe White, maybe Hispanic child.

While in Nigeria, my father owned a tropical fish business. Practically overnight he earned a great reputation. He sold to high-profile and wealthy people (Nigerians and ex-pats). Owning tropical fish isn't a hobby for the socio-economically challenged. His clients included business owners, journalists, those in the President's cabinet and the first President of Nigeria himself: Benjamin Nnamdi Azikiwe (October 1963 to January 1966).

My father loved being in the thick of politics. It wouldn't be long before he wasn't *just* selling the President tropical fish for his terrarium, but was invited to sit in on private meetings between the President and his cabinet members.

Thanks to my father's business, life was great for my family. My mother had her own driver (she never did learn to drive); we had two full-time housekeepers, a cook (whom my mother often kicked out of the kitchen because she loved cooking) and a full-time nanny. His name was Anthony. I don't remember him, but my brothers do and they loved him so much!

## Meanwhile, Back in the Post-Colonial Reality of Nigeria

*The wave of anti-colonialism sentiment that swept across Africa during the post-World War II period was an unstoppable force that no European power could hope to resist. But that didn't stop them from doing everything in their power to retain their influence on the continent, even as the independent dominoes tumbled one after another.*

*Cold War politics brought the United States and the Soviet Union into the picture as well, as both sought to spread their influence (and halt the expansion of the other's), adding further uncertainty into an already volatile situation. Consequently, international intrigue and covert meddling in African affairs continued unabated, and it was against this backdrop that Nigeria gained its formal independence from the British Empire on October 1, 1960.*

*In many of the newly independent nations of Africa, ethnic, linguistic, religious, tribal and cultural divisions threatened the cause of unity, and right from the beginning, such fissures plagued Nigeria's move for self-determination. The Igbo (pronounced "Ebo") people from the east, Yoruba people from the west and Hausa and Fulani peoples from the north were only able to coalesce as a loose federation of states, and when the more populous northerners came to dominate the central government, future conflicts were inevitable. Religious differences between east and north—the Igbo were Christian while the Hausa-Fulani were Muslim—only served to ratchet up tensions and suspicions even more.*

When national and regional elections in 1964 and 1965 were marred by accusations of corruption and fraud, tensions reached the boiling point and a descent into chaos loomed. Two military coups—the first led by Igbo army officers and the second by an alliance of military officials from the north and the west—were supposed to bring order but instead unleashed a torrent of violence, most of it directed at Igbo civilians living in the north.

Following a series of massacres, more than a million Igbo fled to their traditional homelands in the eastern region of the country, creating a refugee problem that was a harbinger of the disaster to come. When the new Federal Military Government under Hausa-Fulani and Yoruba leadership insisted on extending their dictatorial authority over the Igbo people despite earlier promises to grant autonomy, the provisional government in the eastern region (a holdover from the initial military coup) voted in favor of independence, and the incorporation of the new nation of Biafra was announced to the world on May 30, 1967.

With its significant petroleum reserves, relatively prosperous economy, well-maintained infrastructure and high-quality educational system, the eastern region possessed the resources it needed to create a fully functioning nation. But that is what made the prospect of their secession so unpalatable to the Nigerian military junta and the British government that supported it.

The Nigerian government wasn't interested in sharing power or impoverishing its broader natural resource base, while the British weren't about to relinquish the control they maintained over the country's oil supplies through its public-private subsidiary Shell/British Petroleum. The United States and the Soviet Union also backed the Nigerians, fearing Biafran independence might set off a chain reaction that would split sub-Saharan Africa apart at the seams and ultimately undermine the interests of both countries in the region.

*An indifferent international response to the Biafran cause gave Britain a free hand to fund and arm the Nigerian side with impunity. Much of this support was kept secret, but it emboldened the Nigerian military junta, which knew that no level of atrocity was enough to pique the conscience of its British patron saint—or the United Nations for that matter, controlled as it was by the veto power of the United States and the Soviet Union.*

*With no peacekeepers to intervene and no economic boycotts to keep them in line, the Nigerians surrounded Biafra on all sides, squeezing the little upstart nation like a boa constrictor. They instituted a devastating blockade of food, medicine and other essential supplies that was designed to depopulate the Biafrans into submission.*

With connections at the *New York Times* (my godfather was the correspondent for the West Africa region from 1961 to 1967), my father began working with the U.S. Department of State to thwart the efforts to starve the Biafrans. In so doing, although we continued to live in Lagos, he worked closely and became friends with newly minted Biafran President, Chukwuemeka Odumegwu Ojukwu.

In addition to working diligently to circumvent the blockade, my father enlisted the help of several of his wealthy clients to airlift as many as 100 Biafran children out of Biafra. Some were placed into orphanages and others were adopted by Western families. Perhaps the latter was not culturally ideal; however, those were 100 children who wouldn't die of starvation.

Reaction from the Nigerian government was swift. On August 1, 1967, my father, mother and their three children—ages three-and-a-half, two-and-a-half and eight months old—were handed one-way tickets back to the United States. My godfather and his family were also deported around the same time.

## Starting Over in the U.S.

Stateside, my father was more determined than ever to help the Biafrans. He continued working with the Department of State, going back and forth between New York and Washington, D.C.

Shortly after we moved back to New York, my mother started putting pressure on my father to cease his involvement with the Biafran civil war. She had long since realized the Biafrans would be starved into submission. Although she was sympathetic, my father had three children of his own, and we all needed him—at home.

Another impossible situation for my parents. No matter what my father did, it was the wrong decision.

Torn, my father couldn't choose. His loyalty was—of course—to his family. However, his conscience told him he had to help the starving children of Biafra, casualties of ruthless politics.

My mother eventually did it for him, and in March 1969 she asked for a separation. Reluctantly, my father left our apartment on the Upper West Side of Manhattan and moved eleven blocks away—so we three kids could see him whenever we wanted. I was two and a few months when they separated.

While it may seem my mother was being selfish and unsupportive, I never believed that about her. I liken it to the analogy of being on a plane next to a person who needs assistance. The airline attendants always say, "Put your own mask on first, and then assist the person next to you."

## Criminal Mistakes? Now Why Hadn't My Parents Thought of That?

In June 1969, my father's father visited him at his apartment. Having heard from my father's brother that my parents had separated, he needed to verify this in order to reconsider his stance on disowning my father.

"Where's the nigger?" he asked my father.

"Her name is Emily, and you already know she and I are separated. You wouldn't be here otherwise," my father replied.

"Are you planning to divorce her?"

"We just separated a couple of months ago. I realize this is important to you, but can you give me some time to deal with this without coming over here to gloat?"

"Oh, don't tell me you're not over her yet! I swear this Negro has some kind of hold on you, doesn't she?"

My father decided to change the subject before asking his father to leave. "Did you know that I have three children?" As the word "children" left his mouth, my father had already picked up a photo off the coffee table to show his father the grandchildren he'd never met nor would ever express any interest in knowing.

One has to wonder why my father bothered showing his father our picture. For a sensitive and caring person, or even someone who realizes he's filled with hate and wants to make up for it, the obvious response would be something along the lines of, "Oh! They're beautiful. I'd love to meet them," or, "Wow! Look what I've missed!" or, "I am so sorry I have been such a jerk! I want to make it up to them."

Not being any of those, because that would require a shred of humanity, instead his father said, "Your brother told me about the Criminal Mistakes, yes. For some stupid reason your mother wants to meet them. If you had had kids with Barbara, things would be different, but since you had kids with the nigger, I don't need you to introduce me to your Criminal Mistakes."

"Father, you are a hateful person. You have the ugliest heart I have ever seen in a person. Please leave and don't ever come back or contact me." My father showed him the door and that was the last he saw of his father until his father was on his deathbed...at the age of 103.

The epitaph my father and uncle had engraved on their father's tombstone was, "Only the Good Die Young."

## The Black Panthers and the End of the Biafran Genocide

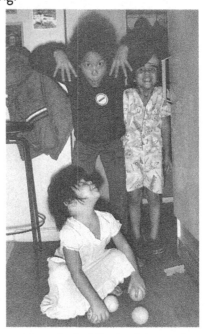

About a year after my parents separated, my mother met a man named Al Brown who was a member of the Black Panther Party.

*The Black Panther Party for Self-Defense was formed by Huey Newton, Bobby Seale and four other young men in Oakland, California in October of 1966. The ostensible reason for the Party's creation was to counter police brutality by providing protective service to the city's Black citizens, but right from the beginning the Black Panthers had a far larger agenda.*

29

*The late 60s were dominated by revolutionary fervor and ambitious political activism, and at that point, the future of capitalist society and the police state that supported it seemed up for grabs—at least in the minds of many young people. In retrospect, those feelings may have been driven more by wishful thinking than reality, but the winds of change were blowing at hurricane speeds and it was clear transformation in society was underway.*

*A revolutionary situation demanded a revolutionary response, the Panthers believed, and they hoped to seize the moment by pushing African American activism in a more radical direction. Black empowerment was their everyday philosophy—and their existential stance—but revolutionary socialism was their motivation for political action. Principled to the core, the Panthers refused to abandon their ideological orientation or sacrifice their deeper principles for the sake of expediency. Some might suggest this was one of the reasons for their downfall (which was brought about more by police-state subversion than anything else), but it is also the reason they are remembered still today.*

*The Black Panthers were bold, assertive and outspoken, taking the critique of racist culture that began in the Civil Rights Movement to a whole new level.*

*The Panthers carried themselves with an edge, lightening-in-a-bottle-style: from six members in one city, Party membership grew to over 400 in less than two years, and by the end of 1968, they had more than 5,000 members in forty-five chapters spread all across the nation.*

*Still unwilling to accept the successes of the Civil Rights Movement and the activism it spawned, the agents of racism and the police state reacted to the arrival of the Panthers on the scene with alarm, hostility and violence. The country's chief law enforcement officer, the malignant and sociopathic FBI director J. Edgar Hoover, famously referred to the Black Panthers as, "the greatest threat to the internal security of the country."*

This announcement coincided with Hoover's covert launching of a counterintelligence operation designed to discredit the Panthers and provoke them into violent responses to police harassment and persecution. Local police departments across the country shared Hoover's racially-tinged contempt for this new radical challenge to the status quo, and from 1967 through 1970 there were a number of shootouts between the police and the Panthers that led to the deaths of at least two dozen young African American political activists.

The police were never charged with a crime in any of these incidents. Not even in Chicago, when a forensic examination following a bloody raid on Panther headquarters revealed the cops had fired more than ninety shots at a half-dozen people (including local leader Fred Hampton, who was executed in his bed). Only one of whom was armed, and that individual only managed to fire off one shot, likely during a death spasm since evidence indicated he had been killed in his sleep.

Most of the Panthers who died at police hands were ambushed and gunned down in a flurry of bullets, either when they were unarmed, not resisting or ready to surrender. As a part of the harassment, numerous Black Panthers were arrested on trumped-up murder or conspiracy-to-commit-murder charges over the years, leading to few convictions but putting the Black Power movement on the defensive at a time when its influence was at its peak and most important.

But there was more to the Panther story than revolutionary socialism and battles with the police. As a part of their community outreach program, the Black Panthers set up free breakfast programs for school-age children all across the nation, and at peak efficiency, they were feeding up to 10,000 hungry children on a daily basis. Party members also set up free medical clinics in poor neighborhoods, bringing vital health services to badly under-served neighborhoods. And their efforts to convince gang members to stop *killing each other and unite in the cause for social justice proved wildly successful, as they helped many young men and women re-orient their lives in a more constructive direction.*

*The constant hounding by police, combined with underhanded FBI tactics designed to sow confusion and dissension in Panther ranks, eventually took a heavy toll on the organization, which lost its cohesion and much of its experienced leadership as the 1970s progressed. But at least in the earliest years of its existence, the Black Panther Party remained firm and clear in its purpose, preserving its defiance and its commitment to radical politics in the face of overt prejudice and oppression.*

*The Black Panthers and the Black Power Movement they represented have sometimes been portrayed as a counter-reaction to the peaceful southern Civil Rights Movement of the 1950s and early 60s. But this conception is misleading and simplistic.*

*Black Power was an outgrowth of the social consciousness created by civil rights crusaders, not a replacement for it, and the violently paranoid response of the government and police state actors to the arrival of the Black Panthers was entirely consistent with the reaction that peaceful civil rights activists provoked when they first appeared on the scene.*

*Racial hatred and reactionary fear motivated the Establishment's response to anti-racist activism at every turn, and there was no approach African American reformers—or revolutionaries—could have adopted that would have been received with kindness and understanding. In such a climate, strong, bold and self-assured actions and attitudes were completely justified, and a thoroughly sensible response to the stubborn persistence of individual and institutional racism.*

Al Brown eventually moved in with us, and with my father gone more than he was home, Al took on the role of surrogate father to my brothers and me.

Because my father's personality was always more dominant than my mother's, although I can't say that prior to Al Brown we had been raised to be White, we definitely weren't raised to be Black. At three years old, I had no concept of the tone of my skin, let alone my brothers', my mother's or my father's.

But with Al in the house—and eventually his Black Panther comrades— there was a lot of Black Power sentiment going on. My mother stopped relaxing her hair and let it go natural—which she alternated between an Afro, twisted or in braids. She and Al encouraged my brother Nicholas to grow an Afro, which he kept through his teenage years.

Ben appeared to be taking after our maternal grandfather. With curly hair like mine (a mixture of both our parents' hair) and Asian features, Ben began to resemble our maternal grandfather, but with hair to his waist.

Just as I was as a baby, I was turning into the sometimes White, sometimes Hispanic child. Very fair-complected with curly hair, I was often mistaken for Puerto Rican. By five years old, I began correcting people by telling them I was Black. Nobody really quite knew how to take that. They still don't.

I think the first time I did the "Black Power" salute in grade school, my teachers called my mother for a conference. She was proud of me and at the same time completely unconcerned by my teachers' reaction.

Things were very happy in our home. My brothers have rarely talked about life before Al Brown. All three of us liked Al a lot. We could be ourselves with him. When we were with our father, we didn't always feel the same freedom. It was probably hard for him. Looking back, I wonder whether he was feeling uncomfortable with the transformation in the three of us. Yes, he was always pro-Black in the sense of Blacks having equal rights to Whites, but that's altogether different from his three kids doing the Black Power salute, referring to racist White men as "the Man[4]" and repeating Malcolm X's commonly used motto, "By Any Means Necessary."

Even the most open-minded, pro-Black White man would feel uncomfortable with his kids using expressions that call out White people for their racist behavior. Not that I imagine he disagreed with our feelings, but he being what comes to mind when someone refers to as "The Man," I can see the conflict.

Outside our doors, there was still the movement (both non-violent and by force) marching on, but inside we were too busy embracing our Blackness. We lived in a sort of bubble. We expressed Black pride and we instantly received praise from our mother, Al and, when they were visiting, Al's Black Panther comrades.

## And Back to Biafra

*The unbearable agony of the Igbo people, whose only crime was seeking self-determination in the face of tyranny and oppression, continued for over two-and-half years. Between the war's beginning in July 1967 and its conclusion in January 1970, somewhere between two and three million people living in the eastern region of Nigeria succumbed to the combined effects of starvation, malnutrition, massacre, a lack of clean water and minimal access to medical treatment or medicine.*

*The death toll accounts for somewhere between fourteen and fifteen percent of the thirteen-and-a-half million Biafrans.*

---

[4] "The Man" A slang term that refers to someone in a position of power (the government, one's boss, etc.) whose goal is to keep a particular demographic (usually Black) under control. Frequently associated with White men who have outed themselves as racists.

One small blessing is that the Nigerians and their backers in the British government weren't able to keep what happened a secret. Western photojournalists descended on the scene in droves, and they were tireless in their efforts to reveal the horrifying truth about the Biafran catastrophe—and the evil intentions behind it—to the world. The images of starving children they captured were transmitted across the planet, wrenching the hearts and souls of the compassionate and bringing shame to British and American citizens appalled by their governments' support of Nigeria's starvation-based strategy.

And there is no question that the starvation deaths of Biafra's civilian population, including hundreds of thousands of its children, were intentional and the result of deliberately chosen policy. In the words of one Nigerian government leader, Obafemi Jeremiah Oyeniyi Awolowo, quoted in the June 26, 1969 issue of London's Financial Times: "All is fair in war, and starvation is one of the weapons of war. I don't see why we should feed our enemies fat in order for them to fight us harder."

Fortunately, humanitarian missions and airlifts designed to deliver food and medicine to the suffering Igbo people did meet with some success. Some of these efforts were supported by well-funded non-profit organizations and even some important politicos, including Senator Ted Kennedy in the United States.

Ultimately, Nigerian intransigence and the absolute unwillingness of the governments in the world's most powerful nations to recognize the legitimacy of the Biafran cause, or to insist on an immediate negotiated end to the fighting, made the tragedy that ensued unavoidable.

It has been argued—with some justification—that the prospective Biafran government should have realized the futility of their situation and surrendered sooner, which could have reduced the scale of the catastrophe. And the fears of some that a successful secession in Biafra could have *triggered further destructive warfare and a fracturing of fragile states across the continent may have had some merit.*

*But while there was plenty of blame to go around, it was the Nigerian government, with contemptible encouragement from the British in particular, that chose to deal with the Biafran rebellion by directly targeting a helpless civilian population with tactics that can only be called genocidal.*

If you would like to know more about the Biafran war, I can highly recommend a book called *The Brutality of Nations* by Dan Jacobs[5].

## Let's Try This Marriage Thing Again

In 1973, my parents reconciled. I honestly don't know who called whom, but I suspect it was my father. One might suppose because my mother was part of the race fighting for equality—fighting against the race my father represented—that she would have needed him more than he needed her. But that wasn't the case. As it turns out, during the four years they were separated and the three years she was with Al Brown, she had done something she hadn't done previously: she confronted and then she owned her Blackness.

Sure, my mother looked Black. There was never any mistaking what her race was—well, her almond-shaped eyes meant there was some question, but the eyes just gave people an excuse to call her exotic (which she hated). Without those eyes, she was a Black woman. But on the inside, I am not 100 percent certain what my mother felt. She often said she felt her kids were Blacker than she was.

And so there they were, back together. Things weren't as fun or as free as they had been with Al Brown. With Al, we could explore and embrace

---

[5] http://www.amazon.com/Brutality-Nations-Dan-Jacobs/dp/0394471385

our Blackness; with our father, we had to do this in secrecy. Again, he was comfortable and proud of us, but it's a whole other story for him to have been "down" with the Black Power with which we were identifying.

By five years old I understood the very subtle difference between striving for equality and asserting our Blackness. I think as long as we (all Blacks) go about our business and don't get too uppity, too in your face and demand too much, all is cool, but the minute one of us gets out of line, smack downs occur. Something we continue to see to this day.

Despite the fact that my parents separated for four years, I see everything each accomplished without the other as being interrelated. My mother was coming into her own and discovering who she was. The job she landed before she met my father was not one typically given to a White woman in the 1950s. For a Black woman to have been in her position, this meant speaking, acting and playing the part. When she was with Al Brown, she was encouraged to be whom she wanted to be. She had no choice but to do it—to fight against the establishment, i.e. the Man.

When my father was working to help save the Biafrans, he did so tirelessly and selflessly to the bitter end. There is no doubt in my mind that my father wanted to be there for us, but he was also called to do something much bigger than himself and to act and protect voiceless people—whose tormentors were the same people as those who strived to keep African Americans and other people of color down.

This may seem like a stretch for some, but if you look at it from another angle, who benefits from keeping a certain demographic of people down? And who benefits from keeping the people in a particular nation down (through colonization, slavery or control of their natural resources)? It's the same entity. I have concluded that, while their marriage had to suffer for a few years, each fight was necessary and in the long run, they were fighting on the same side.

They were both revolutionaries and I hold them both in the highest of esteem. Because I was never able to tell my mother how much I respected her for what she accomplished in her short life, I made a point to tell my father after he was diagnosed with prostate cancer. He died in 2002.

From being in love at a time when segregation was the expectation (and in many states, the law), and marrying despite being disowned by my father's father, to fighting the battle against the Man from two different angles, I wouldn't be who I am or see the world the way I do were it not for my parents repeatedly pushing things long past the level of comfort.

## My High School Years and Beyond

I went to a predominantly Black high school. For the first time in ten years, I encountered Black people who were a throwback to my Black Power-influenced youth. Not only were many of my fellow students all about Black consciousness, so too were many of the teachers—both Black and White. It was so refreshing to be able to talk freely and feel acceptance.

Although I had started coming into my Blackness in grade school, by high school, I was out and proud (and yes, I completely get the gay pride mantra!).

The more I embraced my Blackness, the more uncomfortable my brothers became with me. By high school, Nicholas's Afro was gone and his obsession was with running: track team, marathons, you name it. Brown on the outside and no mistaking his ethnicity, I believe he fought against this. The more Black I became, it seems the more ambiguous he became. I know how others perceive him, but I have no clue how he identifies.

My other brother didn't then, and I don't believe he does today, self-identify. If asked, he lists all his races one by one, never owning one more than another. I never really understood identifying Japanese because we weren't raised in a Black, White and Japanese home—simply because my maternal grandfather died when my mother was five years old. I know more about Japan and its culture and history from reading books than I got from my mother growing up.

For my brothers, the idea that the only one of my parents' kids who could be mistaken for White to identify as Black is ridiculous. For that and for many other reasons, we haven't spoken in years.

The way I see it is pretty simple: we can't unlearn what we know. We can't pretend history didn't happen. We can learn to live in the world we live in, but we can't simply live with blinders on. For me not to choose Black means I am living with blinders on, and I can't do that. Even if I wanted to— which I don't—I can't do that.

## You Ain't Really Black!

In August 1994, my mother died suddenly of an aneurysm. I was twenty-seven. With still so much more growing up to do, soon after her death I moved to Washington, D.C. with the hope of finding myself. I did, but not in the way I had anticipated doing so.

Until I could afford my own place, I lived with a roommate named Michelle. "Black, Bold and Beautiful" is how I would describe Michelle. With looks that reminded most people of Cicely Tyson, Michelle frequently turned heads.

Unapologetic, Michelle said whatever was on her mind. Didn't like her candor or how she called things as she saw them? She often alienated people, I'll say that. We had a run-in within a few months of sharing an apartment together.

We'd made plans to meet up after work one day to have dinner together. At the last minute, she called me to cancel with no explanation of why she couldn't make it. Okay, no biggie. I went home, made dinner and watched a crime drama on T.V.

I went to sleep around 10:30 p.m. and Michelle came home well after midnight. The next morning, I saw handouts from the Congressional Black Caucus sitting on the kitchen counter. I thumbed through them over my coffee and cereal.

"Sarah, it was a magical night!" Michelle was suddenly standing next to me.

"Whom did you go with?" I asked her.

"I got a call in the middle of the day from a girlfriend of mine—you don't know her. She said her husband couldn't attend and she asked if I'd like to go. I actually had another ticket and I didn't know what to do with it."

"Why didn't you ask me if I wanted to go? I would have gone. I have always been a fan of Kweisi Mfume [chairperson of the Caucus from 1993 to 1995]." I was ticked off that she'd canceled plans at the last minute and then even more annoyed that she hadn't even considered asking me to go with her.

"Girl, you wouldn't have fit in there. You do know that membership is only open to African Americans, don't you?"

"Yeah, I know that. Why wouldn't I fit in?" I asked.

"Girl, I know you think you are Black, but for real? Girl, you ain't really Black!" She left the room laughing and talking to herself. "Girlfriend, light as she is, thinks she's Black!" The words lingered long after she left the room.

I wasn't sure if I was pissed, confused or embarrassed. Was this really what people thought of me? Was I, as the expression goes, perpetratin' the fraud? When I got to work, I called a friend of mine, Simone, and asked her to meet me for lunch. I needed to understand what was at the heart of Michelle's remarks. I explained our exchange to her and when I was done, she said, "I have five words for you that will sum up what happened to you this morning. Are you ready?"

"I'm ready. Hit me."

"Field slave versus house slave," Simone said.

I thought about it and it made sense. Light-complected slaves got preferential treatment and got to work in the home—cooking, caring for the kids, serving their slave owners meals, etc.—and the darker ones had to spend long hours in the hot sun, doing grueling work.

"Sarah, think about the terms 'high yellow' and 'redbone'. You've no doubt heard the expressions mulatto, Sambo, quadroon, octoroon, the one-drop rule?"

I had.

"Imagine growing up and always hearing your parents drill it into your head that the darker your complexion, the worse off you are. Jobs are more scarce, people make all sorts of assumptions about you—you're a dope fiend, you'll rob folks blind—you know where I'm going with this?" I did.

"It's no wonder there's so much divisiveness within the Black community," I said. Here we were 130 years post slavery and Blacks were still fighting amongst themselves over roles assigned to them by their slave owners. Never mind that we had no control over those roles and never mind that divided we're doing the Man's work. This light skinned, dark skinned thing runs deep.

What could I say to Michelle to have her understand what I had learned that day? Unfortunately, the "you ain't really Black" conversation is one that has repeated itself many times since, and I have concluded it's an uphill battle.

About all that I can say is that it's difficult enough facing racism from other ethnicities, but to face it from Blacks represents the sharpest of blades right through the heart.

In 1996 I met a man who would get me without me having to explain anything to him. Paul grew up in Washington, D.C. but was living in California when we met while he was home visiting his family.

Paul and I have a lot in common. A few among the many:

- Ideology
- Politics
- Music
- Organic farming
- Love for all living creatures
- We both felt—and still feel—we're square pegs in round holes
- Our views on race and gender issues, both of which (in our opinions) stem from politics and religion
- Not fitting in...fully—with either race

There's no mistaking who Paul is. People look at him and know he's African American. Often (not always), when White people meet or encounter him who don't know him, they will have one of two reactions to him:

- Suspicious of him—expecting him to be a druggie, a mugger or even a murderer
- Ignore him and act as if he doesn't exist

Clearly, something about his nerdy exterior doesn't sit well with these folks who make all sorts of erroneous assumptions about him. Unfortunately, he has never really fit in with Black folks either. Into science and math, not into basketball, football or boxing, and with no discernable accent, Paul has many times been told, "You ain't really Black!" by other African Americans.

Why is it that science nerds who speak well and aren't into sports can't be down? Again, we're doing the Man's work for him when we are happy to divide ourselves into groups and with labels he gave us during slave times.

So while we look very different from one another, we get each other. Like my own family, his spans the rainbow as well (unlike mine, both his parents were African American). Worried I would be teased by his family

for identifying Black, despite being so "light, bright and damn near White," they accepted me for who I am, unconditionally.

And what about how White people see me? I think reactions are similar to the teachers I had in grade school who were perplexed when this very fair little girl gave them the Black Power salute. People look at my skin and think that's the end of the story.

Never looking deeper at my features—lips, nose and cheekbones tell a different story than my glow-in-the-dark complexion.

Hair is another story: neither straight nor curly, it's got a mind of its own. Some days it can't decide if it wants to be tight or loose curls, and other days the Irish cowlick is the only obvious thing on my head! Now living in the tropics, I spend more time taming frizz than worrying about curly or limp.

I have had my hair as long as my waist and as short as Halle Berry's. In one year it can go from short to shoulder length, depending on my mood and my patience. But like India.Arie, "I am not my hair." I try not to let it define me, although there are times when I wish it would be White or Black—this in between thing gets old.

## Puerto Rico and the Farm

In 1998, I moved from the D.C. area to California to live with Paul. We were married in 2001. In 2007, Paul and I became fed up with both corporate life and the racism in the United States. Sure, things are better than they were when the KKK were throwing rocks through my mother's window and lynching Blacks just for fun, but I'd hardly say things are exactly peachy in the U.S. either.

Just a few examples of what I am referring to:

- Dylann Roof arrested for killing nine members for a historically Black church in South Carolina.
- In Florida, an unarmed seventeen-year-old named Trayvon Martin was killed walking in a gated community to his aunt's house by security guard George Zimmerman. Zimmerman was acquitted of all charges.
- Don Imus and his "Nappy-headed hoes" "shout out" to the Rutgers' Women's basketball team (in New Jersey).
- "Let's go fuck with some niggers," said eighteen-year-old Deryl Dedmond, Jr. to John Aaron Rice (of Mississippi) just before they viciously beat James Craig Anderson and ran him over.
- Cartoons depicting President Obama (and sometimes his wife Michelle) as apes.
- Sean Bell, Amadou Diallo, Alerta Spruill and numerous other unarmed African Americans who were killed by the police for no reason whatsoever.
- James Byrd, Jr., a Jasper, Texas male who was dragged behind a pick-up truck for three miles—he was alive for most of the dragging.

- Baltimore riots following the death of Freddie Grey (who died in police custody).
- In Cleveland, Ohio, twelve-year-old Tamir Rice was guilty of playing with a toy pistol. For his "crime," he was shot and killed by two police officers. The Grand Jury chose not to indict the police officers.

We fell in love with Puerto Rico in 2008, gave up our jobs and sold our house, and we came here in the hope of both escaping the consuming-all, all-consuming lifestyle and the racism with one move.

We never deluded ourselves. We never believed Puerto Rico to be Nirvana, but two things make this U.S. colony our Shangri-La:

- Everyone looks just like us—mixed with Taino Indian, Spanish and West African, Puerto Ricans range in complexion from lighter than me to darker than Paul
- Nobody gives a crap whether we're still driving the same old car year after year, asking us when we're going to upgrade to a newer model

We are, for the first time in our lives, Paul and Sarah, or more affectionately known as Pablo y Sarita. We don't have to prove anything to

anyone. We don't have to try and fit in with White or Black people. We can talk the way we want, listen to the music we like (which covers everything from classic rock, reggae and salsa to hip hop, jazz and classical), have the interests we have, and raise our goats, chickens, dogs and cats the way we want without people getting all up in our business questioning why we don't do things their way.

I am not saying racism doesn't exist here—it exists everywhere on earth. However, if someone sees Paul or me as being different, they either stare at us—not disapprovingly, but just to be nosey—or they will simply ask us questions, which we're both happy to answer.

We have many, many friends here who treat us like family. We have built a real community of both Puerto Ricans and a few Americans. We live in a rural farming town—which doesn't generally attract Americans.

We are genuinely happy and feel completely free in Puerto Rico.

## Black, White, Japanese, Other or Biracial?

Where do I fit in? This is a question I am not sure I have an easy answer for. It's obvious to me that I am not as accepted or taken as seriously in the Black community as I thought I was. This question of acceptance or need for me "to show ID" before I am taken seriously has led me to question whether I should self-identify as White and then advocate on behalf of African Americans.

But then I always come back to this: Although it may perplex people and even make some uncomfortable, I am not here to make their lives easier at the expense of who I am.

As a result of writing this book and meeting more Biracial people, I have—rather late in life—come to the conclusion that it's okay to be Biracial. People's attitudes toward race are evolving, and while it was once seen as an "either/or" situation, today being Biracial is actually trending.

Continuing to embrace one's monoracial status keeps us all stuck in a perpetual cycle of "White is right!", "Black is best!", "Asians are the smartest!" etc. Ultimately, I believe that it will be mixed race/multiracial/Biracial people who will advance our society forward toward one race: the human race.

# TWO CULTURES PULL AT MY HEARTSTRINGS

Lezel Nel—Namibia

*Namibian, Malaysian, British and Dutch*

Mixed, different, in the middle: does that reflect my attitude? I cannot say that it does. People with mixed boundaries appear to me more passionate...could be a culture clash. What about a genetic clash? Does one inherit both cultures during conception: strong, willful nature of mama with her stubborn determination and the quiet, resilient willpower of her papa?

A traveler by heart, I can feel my spiritual feet taking me across borders and boundaries looking for my roots. I feel the nudge of nature calling me like the whisper of a farmer calling her back to the land. Silence is my cup of tea; I sip it up in luxurious gaps of delight and savor each of nature's silent calls. Is that the thinker inside me moving away from his pasture to reflect about his day's charge, his life work?

My heart warms when I feel the dry desert sand flowing between my toes. I remember tales my mama told me how they travelled along the desert sand to distant settlements when they arrived in the country many years ago. The isolation of the remote places still draws me in; there is something there for me. I have always felt a little bit a like a Strandloper[6] looking for adventures, picking up treasure and foods along the beach shore. But my ancestry line stops there. Why are my nudges pulling me toward other cultures? Could I be more multiracial than I know? Are my past lives pulling at my wings, calling me to different pastures?

I love my country. We had some ups and downs. Don't we still have ups and downs? We hope to sort that out soon, but apartheid has made me bitter. I hate people who still think that way. To segregate us...I was a rebel in my time. I made like I did not see these rules...it was silly to me. Shopping at a window because you are Black or colored and left with only that imposed meager poor selection of goods and services because that was the class your skin color cast you in.

I questioned my Bloemfontein-segregated shopping experience by walking into an all-White shop and started taking items from the shelves. I saw the little window next to the building but ignored it. I felt offended. I said, "I am from Namibia. We don't know this there," which we did not. I can't remember in my youth ever having to shop at a window. With small packets of brown sugar, brown bread and black tea your only options.

I wanted white bread from time to time and white sugar. What is this system that wants me to settle for brown bread only? Ironically, I prefer these days only brown bread; it makes my stomach more relaxed and I am a healthier individual. Is it not ironic that all that white bread and white sugar may have turned out to be not such a healthy option for those colonial

---

[6] South African for beachcomber.

apartheids; it makes me definitely a little constipated when I've eaten too much.

I will always remember Bloemfontein. They did not want to serve these little hotnots[7] coming into the store, but stopped from chasing us out of the store and took our money. I think they did not want to harass us because the lady with us looked a little White. But I was so angry when I got to my car and heard that they turned my Black friend away and that she had to shop at the window. I scorned their town and told them I will never shop there again, that it was a shit rule.

My education feels hampered and full of holes. I think they really screwed us over. Ours only had two options of professional careers to choose from: teacher and banking clerk, that was all. So most adults become teachers, forced into their career paths; many are still teaching. That is all they learned to do at that point. I'm thinking they can't be very happy with that anymore. It did not really help the education system so much with all those disgruntled potential lawyers and doctors having to settle for being teachers.

I think I slept through the apartheid era in Namibia, then I woke up when I got to South Africa with this boiling feeling inside me wanting to hit someone over the head to wake up. The memories are so much. What happened and the violence was so rife it screams inside me that we could hurt each other like that.

A lot has changed. We live better and more together but have wasted

---

[7] A derogatory term for a mixed race person from the Cape area in South Africa.

each other's time for such a long time, with so much catching up to do. I like White people also, so I'm not a cultural racist, but I hate racists' attitudes when they think God created them differently.

I think to myself, of course he created us differently. Is that not the unique story about creation, wanting to know my sister in the crowd and not a sea of faces not knowing who the real person is?

When travelling to Paris once with my cousin, a Frenchman asked us what language we were talking. We said Afrikaans. That left him quite disgusted with us. He wanted to know why we called it Afrikaans and not just Dutch because that was what it was, or was it the association of the apartheid era with Afrikaans still remembered by some? The White Afrikaner oppressors of the time...

Afrikaans: a dialect that developed after the Dutch settled at the Cape, and it has become the language some of us speak in Africa today. And then he had the nerve to tell us we were not Africans. That really annoyed me because I am just as much African as everybody else living here. My mixed skin color disqualified me in his eyes as being African—the misconception that all Africans are Black.

I remarked it was not my fault that the bloody Europeans came to Africa and impregnated our mothers. Forgive me, Papa. I guess you came for your wife in Africa too. I still like to use these remarks when I hear the White supremacists in America go all superior race on me. "You are not White, my dears. Your grandfathers had affairs with the young slave girls in your households and that is how the American race evolved." Not all mixed babies turn out colored or half Black, and some actually stay White.

I am an outspoken person and when I want to bring my point home, I will find a platform to speak. Growing up as children, I found that our opinions and attitudes were suppressed, as if we had to keep quiet because our opinions did not matter.

My childhood dwindles into a diminished state of Alzheimer's, as if I should not remember who I was and what I did. I only remember little pieces of my childhood, as if someone is holding the rest hostage and it is suppressing me that I cannot remember everything about my life and why should I not.

Two cultures pulling at my heartstrings—I am a spirit that feels I have travelled across countries and gotten to know many cultures, loving all their unique intricate lifestyles. I've made my culture anybody's culture; call me a lover of culture. I can hear them talking, "She is so different," and it makes me want to scream, "Why are you so complacent with your status quo? It should be unsettling!"

Two mixes forming a storm inside me, I can feel my ancestors pulling at my roots: a clash of cultures building up inside my mind, becoming unsettled in my environment looking for my kindred spirits.

At times I feel like a Khoikhoi[8] wandering along the desert sands, seeking wildlife and fresh water, pulling me to desolate pastures following tranquil spaces.

Then I want to be an explorer, looking for new adventures or settlements, learning new cultures, understanding the joy of travel and settling in a new village and appreciating the introduction to new people. We called my mama a Black girl, although she looked like an Asian with European style, and my papa a White man conquering the wilderness in Africa looking for his bride. Are my roots calling me?

---

[8] A member of any of a group of Khoisan-speaking pastoral peoples of southern Africa.

Lezel Nel is Namibian and lives in Windhoek. She is the by-product of British and Malaysian descent on her mother's side and Dutch on her father's side. Her first book, *Camargue My Love*, is available on Amazon.

Camargue My Love:
http://amzn.to/1li8k5z

# SHE IS SO BEAUTIFUL...IS SHE ADOPTED?

## Sarah Degnan Moje—United States

*Irish, Italian and Scottish; Mother of Irish, Italian, Scottish and Puerto Rican child*

"Abby, please come here. It's time to brush your hair." And so begins my morning each and every day; the struggle of wills between my daughter and me as I try in vain to tame her beautifully wild, corkscrew black curls. I get one or two swept up with her *Toy Story* or *Frozen* clips, and five more curls spring out from my grasp. Abby is patient for a moment or two, and then, as with most three year olds, she becomes distracted and squirmy. The fault here is mine, for her pale-skinned, blue-eyed, fair-haired mother has not had much experience when it comes to caring for and styling her exotic Spanish curls. And this is just one minor challenge of being a single mother to my beautiful, Biracial daughter.

From the moment I learned I was pregnant, I knew I would be doing this alone. My child's father is not in the picture, nor will he ever enter into the picture. I am lucky to have a family who supported me and my decision after he chose to turn his back on us, and my daughter is lucky to be surrounded by aunts, uncles and most importantly, a set of grandparents who see her

 for how truly special she is and who more than fill any void left by an absent father. And yet, her father, although he is absent from her life, is present in her features, her dark eyes, her curling hair, her olive skin, and her wide sparkling smile. My ancestry is Irish, Italian and Scottish. I sunburn easily, my light brown hair can be tamed in

five minutes with a blow dryer and my eyes are ocean blue. Abigail is descended from me, and yet, with that extra addition of Puerto Rican, she has inherited not one of my physical traits. That is more than fine with me; she is perhaps the most beautiful child I have ever laid eyes on. People stop on the street to exclaim over her! Strangers ask if she has done any modeling! A photography studio offered us a free session just because she is so photogenic and adorable. All of these are the positives and they are just beginning. I have no doubt that she will grow into a stunning young woman.

And then there is the other part of it—the questions, the glances from her to me and back again. I can see the wondering in people's eyes before the question forms on their lips. And, the questions are always preceded by insults disguised as compliments. "She is so beautiful...is she adopted?" Now, I know I am not Miss America material, but why the assumption that

I could not possibly have produced this beautiful little girl? Or then there is the even more hurtful, "You are so lucky. She's beautiful. She must look just like her father." Zing! A verbal shot to the heart.

And that, more than most other things, is what I fear most for my little one as she grows older and enters into the age of teasing. I am an adult, and these cloaked questions hurt me, even as I deflect them. But, what will happen to her when some older kid on the playground asks why she is so tan or why she does not look like her mother? Even in this day and age, when school-age children are aware that families are different and that some children have no mother or no father, or have a combination of parents and step-parents, there is still that question that young children feel necessary to ask, and the thought that constantly preys on my mind is how best to prepare Abby to answer. At night, each night, before she goes to sleep, I tell her over and over, "You are your mommy's girl. You and mommy both love to smile. You and mommy both love to read. You and mommy both love..." and I fill in the blank with whatever is in the forefront of her little mind that day. I reinforce constantly that she is mine, that she and I do belong to each other and that she was a part of me from the very beginning.

I also, as her mother, make sure that she and I celebrate all aspects of our heritages, the ones we share and the ones we do not. Abigail will wear shamrocks on Saint Patrick's Day and might wear a Scottish kilt to her pre-school's cultural day event. From her first holiday season, when she was only four months old, she celebrated Christmas and Three Kings Day (a holiday celebrated throughout Latin America, which acknowledges the first time the three wise men came to meet Jesus, following his birth), and we always make Three Kings Cake for all the members of our family. I look for books with Irish stories, Spanish stories, Italian stories and Scottish stories. And then, I look for storybooks that have even more of a variety of children and cultures in them. My daughter will grow up to be proud of her beauty, her heritage, her mix of cultures and her Biracial status.

Whenever I grow too worried about her lack of a father, or take mean comments too seriously, or feel that I am just not doing a good enough job raising her to appreciate all the beauty inside her, I remind myself of one very important fact. I took Abby to Disneyworld when she was twenty-three months old. I took her again this past summer when she was almost three years old. Both times, hands down, her favorite ride was "It's A Small World After All." That merry little boat ride, with dolls singing in their native tongue, celebrating not only their uniqueness but what they all have in common, never struck me as more important than when she and I rode it together. All races, all cultures have more similarities than differences. I just have to maintain that "small world" in her heart and in mine and together, we can always face the world smiling as a beautiful, biologically connected, unique mother and daughter who love and appreciate each other.

Sarah Degnan Moje is the single mother of a lively little girl. When Abigail does not have her playing the role of Anna in *Frozen*-themed games, Sarah's full time job is the role of Academic Dean at Saint Dominic Academy, an independent Catholic school for girls in grades 7-12 in Jersey City, New Jersey. She holds a BA in English Literature and a M. Ed in Education and is certified to teach grades K-5 and 9-12. She also holds a certificate of eligibility in School Administration and Supervision.

In addition to her position at Saint Dominic Academy, Sarah works as a freelance educational consultant for New Jersey Teacher to Teacher and does educational writing for Bright Hub Education, LLC. She is also a Regional Council Member of the College Board Middle States Regional Council.

# YOU ARE NOT THE COLOUR OF YOUR SKIN

Søren Kaneda—Canada

*Asian and Scandinavian*

My cousin and I are ordering *schwarma* from the sole Turkish stall in the city when the brawl breaks out. Five Black teens, maybe North African, are getting beaten up by a group of White kids, maybe twenty years old. The groups separate without anyone getting killed and the immigrants back off and then one of the White kids takes his shirt off and throws a *Heil Hitler* salute and I am reminded that yes, I am in rural Scandinavia. I'm remembering that my cousin, despite completing military service, probably doesn't know how to fight, and although I am bigger than most of the kids in the group, it's doubtful that we can win if it comes to that.

I'm jacked up, the fear priming my muscles for something I don't want to do and that's when I am reminded that being half-White is not the same thing as being White.

I am in the country of my birth, a land whose blood courses through my veins, and once again, I am a stranger, a man looking from the outside in. It does not matter where you go. Belonging is something that exists inside of your head. It's not real.

I am in bed, and the girl covers the right side of my face with her hand, revealing the side with the double eyelid. "White," she says, smiling. She switches hands, covering the left side, and now it's the monolid that's staring back at her. "Asian," she says.

## Biology is full of metaphors

The girl, who is from Seoul, was born long after Korea's first exposure to the Biracial. The "real" first generation was generally perceived to be the spawn of American soldiers and Korean prostitutes, and was treated as such. Years earlier, I came across a photo of a couple of these boys taken in the 1960s from an orphanage.

Three Biracial children stare at the cameraman, who's caught them unfiltered. I remember being transfixed by the picture. Their eyes cut right through you. You could see the shame and hatred, the distrust. They knew they were unwanted. They became living ghosts of the past, ostracized since birth. Mistakenly thinking I was part of the first "real" generation of hapas, I was struck by how prototypically "half" their features were: a characteristic blend of East Asian and European facial structures that I'd recognize in an instant.

In a generation, those same faces would appear on runways and billboards across Asia. It's still incredible to me how, in the span of several decades, a group of people could rise from a reviled to fetishized status. Then again, such is the power of White Supremacy, the mimetic mind virus that propagates itself around the world, trailing in the wake of globalization.

Months later, when we are still together, the same girl tells me she's not attracted to Asian men, and I almost choke on my own laughter.

Life is trying to tell you something. It's not that your sense of disorientation isn't real, it's that you're one of the few people with your eyes held open. The circumstances of your birth have forced you to ask yourself a question that few others ever will: are you the colour of your skin?

On some level, I've always been disgusted by the concept of ethnic pride. I've always thought this form of ethnocentrism a kind of weakness, an inability to determine your identity for yourself. If your identity is contingent upon your membership to a group, you are subjugating your individuality to the conformity of the masses. It's a form of exchange, a form of brusque tribalism. We are living in the twenty-first century now, and we don't need these vestigial artifacts.

Ask yourself: who are you?

If your answer is something along the lines of "ethnic pride" (whatever the hell that means), then I have a hard time differentiating that between wearing a bright red jersey and getting into a drunken brawl with some idiot wearing different colours in the stands of the stadium.

Your ancestors are already dead. You don't get to assume credit for their achievements. This form of chest thumping just doesn't make sense. It's not even wrong, it's nonsensical. You are not them, and they are not you. If you're going to bleed for something, bleed for an idea. Bleed for the people you love. What really defines a human being is the sum total of the choices they have freely made. Not the things imposed upon them by genetic chance, social constructs or fate. If you allow yourself to be defined by imposition, that's a form of slavery. Ethnocentrism is a form of imposition, embedded within it a set of cultural expectations about what you can and cannot do. Ultimately, only those things self-determined are of any true value, because those are things you chose for yourself.

What do you believe? How do you live? Who do you love? How did you love them? What did you do with your time here?

Maybe I'm ascribing powers of self-determination to a human being that are overly idealistic. Arguably, we do not have such unrestrained abilities: like a dog attached to a leash, we are bound by the causal constraints of our past. But that's the very purpose of an ideal: something to reach for, something aspirational. And within that limited space is still a kind of freedom. I catch myself lionizing the achievements of half-Asian people all the time. That's the kind of pull my monkey brain exerts on me, dragging into this lower form of consciousness.

Maybe the scientists are right. Maybe the scientists and computer models are right: maybe racism had some type of genetic game-theoretic advantage in our evolutionary past. Maybe that's why it's such a universal problem. The correct response isn't to be disturbed—it's to be indifferent. Why should we be constrained by the past? Who cares?

Were primates supposed to fly into space?

That sense of displacement you have, because you're from two different worlds? Don't curse it. It's not that you don't belong. You've been given something else instead. You've been granted the freedom to choose who you want to be. No—this freedom has been foisted upon you. You cannot choose either side because you are not merely one of your two halves—you are both, and you are neither.

You are the choices you have made, and nothing else.

Søren Kaneda is half Asian and half Scandinavian. A resident of Vancouver, Canada, he is currently working on his first novel.

http://www.sorenkaneda.com

# MY DAUGHTER IS DILUTED

## Jamie Frayer—United States

*Black and White; Mother of Black and White child*

I thought I had resolved my identity issues, adulthood bringing a confidence that was denied me in youth. I had become pretty comfortable in my skin, literally and figuratively. That was, until the birth of my daughter.

## All babies are not cute

This is particularly true for the first few weeks of life. When I was finally given the opportunity to really hold and look at my newborn, the first thoughts that ran through my head were: She is funny-looking. And wrinkly-faced. And hairy. And White.

Now, I knew enough about basic life sciences and the miracle of childbirth to realize that the purple, wrinkly-faced, simian-like features would go away with time, and she would soon blossom into that cute bundle-of-joy moms rave about. I also knew that unless I roasted her like a turkey in the sun for a few hours a day, she would not be getting any darker, and that realization bothered me.

Why was her race important? Why was it that one of the first things I thought, and would later say aloud, was that I had given birth to a little White girl? Her race shouldn't have been a surprise to me. My husband is White. My mother was White. My skin color, for all intents and purposes, is White. I learned basic genetics in high school biology; of course I would give birth to a White baby. But I'm not White, and on August 19, 2010, looking at the life I had created, I felt a burning need to remind the world and myself that I was not White and neither was my little girl.

Well, I am White. And Black. And who knows what else; the family stories are many and varied. I am a mongrel, a mutt, a half-breed, a Heinz 57. I'm mulatto, Biracial, mixed. I am all of these things and none of these things.

I grew up in the 1980s, raised by my father, a single Black man. Single fathers with primary or sole custody are rare in 2015; in the 1980s they were almost unheard of[9]. Finding a

household with minor children headed by a single Black man would have been like finding the elusive giant squid we all know exists but haven't been able to capture.

I'd never considered the differences between my dad and me. My father was one of five children, each of whom had vastly different

---

[9] Pew Research Center: The Rise of Single Fathers
http://www.pewsocialtrends.org/2013/07/02/the-rise-of-single-fathers/

skin colors, hair textures and facial features. Theirs was a diverse family, and one I assumed to be the norm.

My aunts were "high-yellow"—Aunt Karen easily "passed" for White, and Aunt Nancy had natural blonde hair and blue eyes. The three boys were all brown-skinned, but my Uncle "Bunky" had hypnotizing hazel eyes and hair that was too fine to support an Afro. My grandfather was very fair-skinned; rumor had it he was mixed. And based on photos (and his offspring) it's safe to assume those rumors are true.

So, you see, I thought it didn't matter, the color of my skin. That's what I had been taught by my family and in my history class. It didn't take long for me to learn otherwise.

It is rumored that my grandmother, a brown-skinned woman, was accepting of my birth—which had been rooted in controversy unrelated to race—because I was "light enough." She believed her progeny would have an easier life if they could "pass." *Colorism*, prejudice based on the variation in skin color within a race or ethnicity, has long been a problem in the Black community. Many attribute this divide between light-skinned and dark-skinned Blacks to slavery and the preferential treatment given to mixed-race slaves, usually to special treatment paid to offspring of a plantation owner.

While my grandmother was thrilled with my light skin, "good" hair, and hazel eyes, my peers were not so accepting. I was always too Black for the White kids and too White for the Black kids. What exactly is "too Black" or "too White"? Thirty-seven years of walking this invisible line, and I'm still not sure.

I identified as Black. I was raised by a Black man, went to predominantly Black schools, and was surrounded by Black people and Black culture and Black experience. Yet, I found my Blackness constantly on the attack. I'm sure my outward physical appearance had a lot to do with it. I was probably viewed as a perpetrator, a "wigger," someone trying to be something I wasn't. Thanks to the popularity of "urban street wear" designers, rap and hip-hop music, and increased media representation, Black culture had become trendy by the 1980s and 1990s. Suspicion of me and anyone else who did not LOOK black was understandable.

When you're constantly forced to defend something about yourself, you eventually begin to question the very thing you're defending—like an innocent man who confesses to a crime after hours of relentless interrogation. When you receive so many messages contradicting what you know and believe, it can be hard to remain true to yourself, especially for a young woman just coming into her own.

Life eventually led me away from the big city, with all its diversity and acceptance. I landed in a small, semi-rural, very White town and was introduced to a whole new set of racial issues. For the first time in my life, I heard the word "nigger" spoken aloud. (Don't get me wrong; I grew up using "nigga" as a term of endearment, the merits of which are debatable.) I had watched enough documentaries to have heard the word, but never had I experienced the use of it by a real life human being with the intent to demean or degrade. And I had read about the Ku Klux Klan, and in my naiveté, thought them long gone. But there they were: alive and well in my new town, holding annual rallies on the courthouse steps. The confederate flag waved proudly from porch roofs, and could be seen everywhere on truck beds, caps and t-shirts.

Rarely was this ignorance directed toward me; as I said before, I "passed." But this fact did not soften the blow or minimize the hurt when rancid racist words, thoughts and imagery did appear.

Thankfully, the Black community in this new town was much more accepting of me than those in my native Pittsburgh, Pennsylvania. I think when there are so few of you—three percent of the total population—skin color ceases to be a divisive factor, and shared experiences become a binding thread. I met young people who looked like me and shared similar circumstances, and I was accepted into a small, close-knit community of supporting and empowering individuals. It was through these new friends in a new town that I found the confidence to be me. Black me. White me. Nigger me. Mulatto me. Half-Breed me. Just ME.

I learned that the sum of my experiences had made me into an open, empathetic, independent, motivated and determined woman, and that the color of my skin or of people's reactions to it was simply not my problem.

For years I lived in a euphoric racial bliss. I no longer cared whether I made someone uncomfortable because I did not fit their preconceived notions of what a Black person should look like or how a White person should behave. I matured personally, professionally and spiritually. I could honestly say I loved myself.

Then I got pregnant.

I had never dreamed of being a mother; as a kid, baby dolls weren't for me. I didn't plan elaborate weddings and hope for white picket fences, two point five kids and a dog. But there was one thing I was certain of: if (and that was a very big "if") I had children, the father of said children would be the darkest, Blackest man I could find. My children would be Black and there would be no doubt or question about it. Period.

It turns out, of course, that my partner of thirteen years, my best friend and soul mate is White—small town, pick-up-truck-with-oversized-tires White. And he is the father of my child.

For the first two years of her life we raised our daughter without mention of race because it didn't seem to matter. Despite my delivery room musings, race did not matter for her because it did not matter for me. Right?

Then Travyon Martin happened. And Mike Brown happened. And Eric Garner happened. And Tamir Rice happened. A national debate on race in

America was reignited. I learned a lot about what my "friends" and family thought about race, race relations, and the legacy created by the ugliness that was 200 years of slavery.

I also learned a lot about my own ideas on race, and had lots of opportunities to reflect on my experiences as a child and an adult. What I realized is that no matter how much we say, or dream, or do, race matters. It matters in very big ways. Race is so tightly woven into our history as a nation and a people that it has to matter. To ignore it is to ignore what this country was founded on and what it is destined to be.

I think it was easy for my White friends to forget that I was Black. I made it easy for them. My skin made it easy. I intentionally left the slang and street cred at home with my roots. I had worked so hard to feel comfortable and to make others feel comfortable that I'd spent years hiding the person I was and am and will always be.

I've joked that my daughter is diluted—made a mockery out of raising a "little White girl." In doing that I've made a mockery out of myself and my childhood and all the experiences that come together to form the essence of me.

Today all of the ignorance and foolishness that I've been pandering to is coming to an end. I will raise my child as an American and only an American. She is not White or Black or Latina or Asian, or Other, or any of the many attempts to classify and categorize, ultimately dividing the very people asked to pledge allegiance to a nation that is "indivisible with liberty and justice for all." I will raise my daughter to know, love, and embrace her history, her culture and her experiences. I will raise my daughter to learn about, respect, and empathize with the varied experiences of those around her.

I only hope that I do a better job of it than was done for me.

Jamie Frayer was born and raised in Pittsburgh, Pennsylvania. She is Biracial, born to a White mother and a Black father. Jamie is also the parent of a Biracial daughter, as her husband, Tim, is White.

They live near Erie, Pennsylvania, where their daughter is now five years old and about to start kindergarten. She owns a business called Precision Executive Services (http://www.precisionexecutiveservices.com), which offers operational, personal and executive level administrative support to busy entrepreneurs.

When Jamie is not making her clients' lives easier, she and her family love taking spontaneous road trips. A bit of a geek, Jamie finds pleasure in creating and manipulating Excel spreadsheets and Access databases.

# ON BEING EVERYONE AND NO ONE

Janek O'Toole—Australia

*English and Sri Lankan*

I became aware of the complications of race in my life when I was five. This was when I started pre-school, which meant it was also the first time I was surrounded by other children whose skin was a different colour to mine. Evidently frustrated by my inability to blend into the masses, I declared to my mother, "I want to be White, like dad." To which she responded by pointing out that my father was called "White" but was, in reality, a fairly vivid shade of pink, and asked if that was what colour I wanted to be. That was the first and last time I voiced any preference for the colour of my skin. But it wasn't the last time I wished my skin were a different colour.

I live and was born in Australia to a Caucasian English father and a Sri Lankan Sinhalese mother. I have an Irish last name and the Czech derivation of a French first name. What I'm saying is, I am as confusing as a person could possibly be when it comes to race. Like most children of Caucasian-South Asian parents, my skin's the pale brown people used to associate with Hispanic people and now associate with people who commit acts of terror. Indeed, between my skin colour, hipster beard and what appears to be a poorly thought-out fake name, I'm everything the world's intelligence agencies are looking for when setting up a date for their lonely waterboards. It may seem glib to make light of what is a serious situation, but being mistaken for an Islamic extremist has been something I've had to get used to ever since 2001, when I had to skive off school for a week because the bullying over what "my people" did became too much.

But the interesting thing about being multiracial is that when you stand out from the mainstream, you kind of fit in everywhere else. When I was nineteen, I went on a holiday to Europe with my parents. We went to England to visit family, then France, Spain, Portugal, Italy and Greece. Over the course of that trip across continental Europe, I became Spanish, Portuguese, Turkish, Italian (northern Italians insisted on making me specifically Sicilian), Greek, Cypriot, Romani and Algerian. Oh, and in England, I was twice called a "Paki[10]," so I was that too.

Here's how invested the Portuguese were in my being a local. When we arrived at the airport in Lisbon, my parents went ahead of me while I waited to get my computer from an overhead locker. As I crossed the tarmac, I was shepherded by security officers into a little pool of people being screened. That's nothing new, when your face is as vaguely Middle Eastern as mine. You become well acquainted with airport security. But what was new was that all the people around me were Caucasian, and I realised that I was the token local! I was the one "Portuguese" person they pulled out to show they weren't racially profiling, that really, everyone gets picked. I still remember

---

[10] Insulting name for person of Pakistani origin.

the surprise on the screening officer's face when I showed him my Australian passport with my Irish last name and my Czech derivation of a French first name. And he still had a crack at speaking to me in Portuguese!

Growing up in Australia where sport is the number one religion, the on-going case of my mistaken identity is a regular occurrence in my life. When Australia was dominating the Bledisloe Cup against New Zealand, there were plenty who decided I was a Maori and that they'd like to tell me all about how rubbish "my" team was. Every time Australia beats a team from India, Pakistan, Bangladesh or South Africa, that's apparently where I'm from for the next week. Bizarrely, this has never, EVER happened when Australia beats Sri Lanka...During the Olympics no one knows what's going on with me; I can only imagine what it'll be like when it's in Brazil, a country famous for people showing off skin the same colour as mine.

But the interesting thing is that whenever someone makes such a mistake, or certainly when they express it out loud, that's never it. It's never, "I wonder if this person's from [insert country I'm not from here]?" It's always because they want to say something about some people, and I'm just the representative of [whatever other country I'm not from] to say it to. The moral of the story is that when people make an assumption about my race, they're saying something interesting about themselves. It's not a racism thing; this isn't a lesson about not judging a book by its cover. That quality is an innate human instinct. However much we try to avoid doing it, our subconscious is evolutionarily wired to do so. And the reality is that both evolutionarily, and in my own life, it's probably been more for the better than the worse.

For every chav[11] who called me "Paki," or Greek who wanted to tell me about the genocide "my people" committed (I was Turkish that time), or

---

[11] British slang for a young, brash lower-class person who wears real or imitation designer clothes.

the French official who was convinced I was a gypsy trying to sneak into their country, there have been so many more Spaniards who wanted to celebrate the 2010 World Cup with me; Portuguese who earnestly wanted to hear my opinion on the state of the economy; and girls who were interested in me only because they thought I was whatever race they'd fetishized in their minds. What people project is either positivity or negativity; they want to be aggressive, so they ascribe to me a race they're comfortable being antagonistic towards, or they want to be positive, embracing or bonded, so they ascribe me to a race with which they'd like to connect.

But of course the reality is we are not connected in that way. An arbitrary assignation of nationality may affect a few moments of interaction, but it does not affect my place in the world. My skin does. As much as I am from everywhere, I am also from nowhere. I am half-Caucasian English, but I'm plainly not Caucasian if I am not privy to the experience of living as a Caucasian, I cannot fully understand what it's like to be inside that culture, and so I am outside. At the same time I am half-Sinhalese, but I am too light, my hair is not black, and my nose isn't quite right. I may be vaguely South Asian enough to convince a stranger passing on the street, but I'm clearly not like my family—I am outside of them. There is an unspoken, unseen barrier that disconnects me from both sides of my family. To the English side, I'm always half Sri Lankan; to the Sri Lankan side, I am always half English. I will never be a whole.

Which turns out to be perfect, because I get to see something no one else gets to see. With one foot in each camp, I am close enough to observe and practice the traditions of each race, but distant enough to think analytically about them. I am Jane Goodall: the world around me is my chimp community. I could never rely on just blending into the background. Any time I did anything different, I stood out, so my skills of observation have been honed through years of growing up observing the people around me—my family, whom I now realise I just likened to apes—to make sure I could copy them so I could fit in as closely as possible. This has both informed and infinitely aided my choice to write professionally. I've had decades' worth of practice observing how people operate and how cultures operate, both internally and interactively. Whether I'm called on to reflect critically on the world—as I am now—or whether I have to guide a character's actions through a piece of fiction, I have a vast index of culturally-specific responses upon which to draw.

And I have a cache on one of the world's increasingly valuable skills: analysis. Critical thought is currency, with all information now subject to higher levels of scrutiny than ever before. The inability to think critically or a lack of talent for it (which once was the norm), are now signs of ignorance or naivety, while the ability to deconstruct the relationship between texts, their creators and their audiences are becoming required skills, particularly online. The difficult lessons learned whilst in the minority (the minority of the minority) have inadvertently seen me flourish as part of a mainstream where such arbitrary assignations as nationality and gender are replaced by more layered and nuanced and—most importantly—self-chosen cultural markers.

Janek O'Toole is half English and half Sri Lankan, and lives in Australia. He has a BA in Media Studies, as well as a diploma in Film Studies from the Australian Film, Television & Radio School. He is a freelance screenwriter and script editor, and has written three short films.

# ETHNICALLY SPEAKING

Anonymous—United States

*Vietnamese and American (White)*

I was born American in an American hospital in Orange County, California in 1982. I can't identify as anything other than 100 percent American. I'm not *Asian*-American. I'm not American-*Asian*. I have a Californian accent and, by nature of upbringing, when I think "American," I automatically think "White." I have a White first name and, though my middle name is derived from my mother's Vietnamese last name, Ly, it has been adjusted to be White: Lynn. If a Hollywood makeup artist adorned me in costume as a White woman, I could go out on the town and none would be the wiser.

*I feel* White. I *act* White. I *think* White. I *am*, for all intents and purposes, White.

But, really, I'm not.

My father, an Army enlistee and native Floridian of mixed European blood, met my mother while serving his two years in the Vietnam War. They courted amidst the turmoil of that nation and were there quietly married by a magistrate. Not long after my father returned to America, my mother went to be with him, crossing an ocean and, once and for all, leaving (or escaping?) the only place she'd ever known.

Like many who survived that conflict, my parents speak rarely of it. My father has little to say about his life in the military but will reminisce every once in a while about his Army buddies and the spicy Thai dishes he loved so much. The two stories that stand out for me involve critters: the first, when he was manning a radio station on a sandy beach and, leaving his post, walked across the sand, the crunch of incalculable insects beneath his feet yielding to his every step, and, the second, the endless nights battling huge geckos infesting his apartment and how he would trap them in the roll-up shade and then discard them (after a killing, of course) out into the night. That's what I think of when I think of my father's Vietnam: spicy food, big bugs, bigger lizards and war.

My mother would occasionally reminisce about the simple times of her youth—like when, as a small child, she climbed a fruit tree during a game of hide-and-seek and, so well hidden, ate the fruit until suppertime came round and she climbed down—but I recall little else from her. Inasmuch as I know, it was not a happy place—an ear infection there marred her hearing for life—and she doesn't express any desire to go back.

My sisters and I attempted to connect with being Vietnamese while growing up. Even today, well into our adult lives, we still try to make that connection in ways that we can, mostly revolving around food: eating phở, making spicy beef salad with cucumbers or yellow curry chicken over jasmine rice. Mom used to shop at an Asian market, and she used to cook Thai and Vietnamese food often. But over the course of time, because she worked hard to fit in, her cuisine has become more and more Americanized; Asiatic dishes are a rarity in her kitchen now, though not forgotten. Each of my three sisters and I tried our hand at learning our mother's language, the youngest of us getting the farthest—counting to ten—but by now the skill is long forgotten. Mommy used to listen to Vietnamese music on cassette tapes, but I haven't heard those ladies singing since my grade school days.

My sisters and I have never been to Vietnam. Our mother hasn't returned since she left. One day, we hope to go there together to strain from it what we can of part of who we are. On that trip, I envision a lot of wonderment, confusion, disbelief, misplacement, memory-making and crying.

But as I said, I *feel* White, though I know I'm not. I only remember that little fact when I meet someone new or when I'm faced with a demographical survey and involuntarily take a pause to think about my answer. I'll opt for White 80 percent of the time, Asian 15 percent and Decline the remaining percentage when I just don't know how I feel about myself. As I left home for school in 2000, I ran into many such forms. My first two friends at university in Arizona, one undeniably Hispanic and one unquestionably Caucasian, couldn't make me out. They'd tease me a little about my heritage, but when I didn't respond to their liking, soon stopped, the fun having gone from the game. When they realized that I knew little of Vietnamese food, culture, holidays, et cetera, I became just "another White girl from California." Subsequent friends, friends-of-friends, boyfriends, neighbors, acquaintances and co-workers have met me with equal wonder and, dare I say, disappointment.

Meeting new people is inevitable. And, I've come to accept the ethnicity question. That is, "What *are* you, anyway?" (Or various forms thereof, such as "What's your background?", "What ethnic mix are you?" or, from the confident ones, "Are you [insert assumed ethnicity here]? You look like you're [insert assumed ethnicity here].")

Answering the question is tiring because I find myself reciting every time the topic comes up: "Yes, my parents met during the War; no, I don't know the language or the culture; no, I've never been there; yes, I'd like to go one day."

The confident inquirers are less draining and somewhat interesting. I've stopped keeping track of the ethnicities I've been associated with: American Eskimo, Spanish, Mexican, Native American, Filipino, Hawaiian, Ecuadorian, Panamanian, among others. The most unique I got was Gypsy, and that was from a store clerk in Romania. The man probably thought I was going to steal something, and I could feel his hawk eyes on the back of my neck. I opted to spend the few minutes my companion spent shopping sitting outside on the front steps.

I don't mind when I'm confused with another ethnic group. In fact, it makes things interesting. If I were more of an actress, I could try playing off the role, but I'm a terrible liar. People's confusion means nothing to me other than that they haven't a clue: they're just guessing. It's no insult. At least they're *trying*. It's only bad when they anticipate I'll have good stories to tell of interesting cultural practices or experiences, of which I have none. We end up lingering quietly for a few seconds in mutual awkwardness until one or the other of us decides upon another topic to discuss.

Mostly, I tire of the ethnicity question because I have no Vietnamese pride to speak of. Not that I am ashamed—heavens, no!—but I don't *know* the place. I have no ties to Vietnam other than through my mother, who considers herself 100 percent American, citizenship and all. I am *American*. I know of and about *America*. My family, true to my mother's culture, ironically, was patriarchal, and my father is White. That's how I identify.

I have had both the privilege and blessing not to have been scarred— though perhaps dinged—by ethnic backlash from any side. I don't pay attention to raised eyebrows anymore. As a college student in the summer of 2002, I was mopping the floor one evening, closing another shift at the Sub Station in Riverside, California, when a young boy around age ten trailed his family out the door. Almost out, he ran back in toward me, stopped a few feet away, used two fingers to stretch his eyelids into slits, then proceeded to grin and make a racist joke about Asians. I stood there, mop in-hand, face blank, unsure of how to take the matter, when his father ran in, having obviously overheard, grabbed his son ashamedly by the collar, forced him to apologize, apologized himself and swiftly left.

I remember that instance mostly because of the reaction of the father, not because of any hurt I experienced from his son's insult. I wish I could know what was on that man's mind as he overheard the joke, how his heart skipped with embarrassment as he ran back in, what he said to his son on the ride home, what the boy's mother would say when they arrived.

Me? I just shrugged and kept mopping the floor, relieved that he hadn't run in to kick over my water bucket.

Adults, however, are of three types: those who take the answer and don't dwell on it, those whom I'm a disappointment to and who can't understand why I don't want to know more about my background, and those who wish to teach me what they know. Of these, I acknowledge the first as the only respectable and polite stance to take.

I'm a disappointment in Vietnamese restaurants to those who expect my knowledge in related cultural affairs to be all encompassing. I was most recently frustrated by a woman who encapsulated both the second and third types; a Vietnamese-wannabe, a purely White and petite Minnesotan woman who presumed to teach me, sans request, everything there was to know about being Vietnamese, from food and language to dress and custom. It was dirty, hand-me-down snobbery passed to her by her (ex) mother-in-law. I was not impressed when she tried to impress upon me her wealth of expertise of the language of "my" people, all night asking, "Do you know what *this* is called in Vietnamese? Do you know what the word is for *that*?"

Gag.

I had to contain myself from reaching across the table at her over my fresh bowl of phở and emphasizing that I was *not* Vietnamese, I was *American*, and that she ought to consider taking my lead.

Although I've come to terms with ignorance in all its shades, I consciously try to avoid circles where "sticks and stones" are thrown. Being a cultural mutt of the times, so to speak, people's reactions are usually diluted to a degree mild enough that their presuppositions go easily unnoticed or, alternatively, can be tastefully digested with a grain of salt.

The insult and rage comes when my mother, who has worked so hard to be a part of this country and who loves none other, is downtrodden by my American brothers and sisters. When she is disregarded by haughty Whites who think she is uneducated and incompetent; when she is jerked around by employers because of her appearance; when she is teased by people she knows because of her still-lingering accent; when she is insulted by her own countrymen—fellow Vietnamese—because she isn't being "Vietnamese enough"...

I could choke somebody for that. Even now, as I write this, the anger makes my eyes well and my heart pound.

But, still, even though her pain is caused by discrimination from one side or the other, my reaction is not to defend the Vietnamese race. It's to defend my *mother,* and in that I am not different from any other person, White, Vietnamese, or otherwise.

I never wake up thinking about how I'm a "half-and-half." Truly, I would be surprised if I think of it once a week. But I think upon it deeply when I do, because it is such a true part of me. Who would I be without my mother's

82

influence? Had the Vietnam War not happened, who would I have been born to, if at all?

And I've read about that war, the loss of life, how it changed the United States and divided the people of our great country. I've read about the biological weaponry and seen pictures of what Agent Orange did and is still doing to the Vietnamese children born there today. The sickness and deformities are unimaginable, like something from a science-fiction film, yet so real.

Sometimes I look at those pictures and wish that war hadn't happened. So, yes, sometimes I look at those pictures and wish I hadn't been born.

And I guess that's the thing I want to express. No huge statement about discrimination or identity, but just that: for all the questions and the curiosity and well-meaning inquiries, that's how I feel sometimes when I'm approached about my heritage. I want people to understand the disappointment under that rock they so eagerly peer beneath. It's natural to ask one's ethnic mix and I accept that—but I sometimes wonder if people who aren't half-bloods realize the weight of the stone they're lifting. If they comprehend the deeper conflict that may arise in those being questioned; if they realize there might be things nobody wants to talk about under there, things that bite and sting and can't really be understood.

Half Vietnamese and half Caucasian, this author was born in the early 1980s in Southern California and raised in the heyday of "the fastest growing city in the United States." After earning her BA in the mid-2000s, she married her dream man in the midst of rediscovering herself (a rediscovery which has yet to be concluded).

She currently works as a freelancer from her home in the Midwest (USA). Her family is scattered across the States, spread from the Pacific to the East Coast, from near the Canadian border to the southernmost tip of Texas. She considers herself blessed to have family and friends who are so diverse in their thoughts, races, and ethnicities, and anticipates a Heaven that is equally colorful.

# YOU NEVER TOLD ME YOUR DAD WAS BLACK!

## Heather Rolland—United States

*White, Jewish and Black*

I discovered that I was Biracial when I was seven years old. I walked home from school with Carmen, the local bully, having decided that befriending her was going to be a lot easier than avoiding her since she lived in my neighborhood. I invited her over and while she was waiting for me to pour her a second glass of lemonade, she wandered away. She drifted around my living room, looking at my family's stuff—trinkets and tchotchkes, set out for display on the memory shelf, alongside a family portrait.

"You never told me that your dad was Black!" came the cry from the living room. I set down the glass of lemonade and went to investigate. My dad was many things—Jewish and dead topping the list—but Black was a new one.

Carmen stood in front of the family portrait, slack-jawed and staring. Carmen, I guess I should add, was Black. Up until that moment, I thought I was White. My mom was White, my sister was White...I just assumed I was White. But if my dad wasn't White...then what was I?

Slowly the stories came out over the course of my childhood. The time my mom and dad were dating and they went to a swim club together: "You can't bring him here," hissed the woman in charge of membership to my mom while my dad swam.

"Why ever not?" asked my mom, truly innocent.

"Because he's Black," was the answer.

My mom and dad dated in upstate New York in the late 1950s. It was not a good time to be an interracial couple. My mom is British, red-haired, green-eyed, with milk-white skin that freckles in the sun. She came to this country oblivious to the issues of race and religion. Her parents back home in England had accepted my dad, and my mom saw him as Jewish, not Black. Who knew he could be both?

When I was two years old, my dad's cancer was diagnosed. A tumor in his eye meant that he had to have it removed. He withdrew from family life gradually, as his immune system became more and more compromised. By the time I turned five, he was a ghost in my parents' bedroom, rarely leaving except to go to the hospital. He was thirty-nine and I was five when he died.

How could I not know whether or not my dad was Black? How could this information come as a surprise to me? I stood shoulder-to-shoulder with Carmen, staring at the family portrait along with her, and saw it for the first time through an outsider's eyes. I guess he's Black, I decided.

That was certainly as possible as anything else.

My father had dark skin, a Brillo-pad Afro, and thick lips, but in truth he didn't really look Black, any more than a member of the Hopi tribe looks Japanese. He simply looked different: not White. Where I grew up, White had some variations—you could be Italian, Irish, "American" (meaning your family came to the US a few generations before everyone else's), or like me...half-breed. But not White was not White, lumped into a giant garbage can category of Otherness that meant limits and closed doors. Mom was not supposed to have brought my dad to that swim club. After my dad died, we looked into joining another swim club—the one to which all my neighbors belonged. All my neighbors were White (and perhaps not incidentally, not Jewish). Membership at that club was not available to us. Mom decided to join the town pool instead.

Being half Jewish was as bad as being not White. I wasn't baptized, so if I wanted to pretend to be Christian and go to church (something I flirted with after my father died), that charade could only go so far. If I wanted to embrace my Judaism and attend Hebrew school, I'd have to convert to Judaism since my mom was Christian. I gave both an honest shot and ended up giving up on both religions.

The more I have considered Carmen's words in the four decades since she spoke them, the more I wonder about my own racial identity. I have no word for what I am, no label I can adopt with any integrity. I am not Christian and not Black and not Jewish and not White. The only word that means anything to me is "half-breed," and ever since age seven, that felt ridiculous to adopt.

Why not Biracial? I think the simple answer is because I live as a White person without question. You'd have to see a photo of my father to ask any questions about my race or ethnicity. Sure, I've been asked about Mediterranean heritage: "Are you Italian?" is a common one. Spanish and Puerto Rican have been suggested as well. When I traveled in India, I discovered that as long as I kept my mouth shut, I could pass as native, especially in the north—shopkeepers spoke to me in Punjabi or Hindi on a regular basis, assuming I was a light-skinned Indian woman. I thought nothing of it until I saw a photograph of my grandmother as a child and was astonished to see what clearly looked like a South Asian little girl staring back at me.

After a few months of wandering around India, I would play with the local touts and shopkeepers, daring them to guess my ethnicity. Iranian, Iraqi, Punjabi, Israeli, even Turkish were all frequent guesses. I took great delight in being inscrutable—half British, half Jewish was just not in anyone's lexicon.

I reserve the term Biracial for someone who owns and embodies both aspects of the "bi"—someone who knows who and what they are and lives with that. Someone who has paid the price of being "half Black" in a society that has no idea how to deal with that except to limit, segregate, hate and fear...and misunderstand.

Having lived my whole life as White, I never truly had to deal with that. Yes, we couldn't join the country club, that's true. But even if my dad didn't have an Afro, we still couldn't have joined. No Blacks, no Jews. The reality of anti-Semitism has colored my life (pun intended) more vividly than the race issue.

The price that I have paid is more private, more personal. I never knew my dad. His death leaves a great hole in my heart, and the emotional baggage it left did not fit in my overhead compartment for many years. Coming to some semblance of peace with that has been a long process, supplanted over time by the unanswerable questions and curiosity about his own background.

Why was he so "Black?" Why did my grandmother look Indian? European Jews—the Ashkenazi—look White. My dad's people came from the Ukraine and fled during the pogroms of the early twentieth century (the pre-holocaust extermination campaign that no one really talks about). The Jews from that area at that time were also White. Why my family was different is something I'll never know because nearly all of them are dead, and those who remain wouldn't admit to being anything but White. They call his hair a Jew-fro and say that he was just dark. Period.

About twenty years ago, I was experimenting with ethnic cooking and I came upon a Sephardic recipe for a dish that looked interesting. Sephardic Jews, ethnically speaking, are not European. North African in origin, they fled during the diaspora. The history of the Jews is basically a moving target—you can't ask where they lived so much as you have to ask where they were and where they went once they were kicked out. My grandmother's maiden name was Auslander—German for "foreigner." From North Africa to Spain, the Sephardic Jews were influenced by Spanish culture before they got kicked out of that country and moved on. The likelihood that my father's family was Sephardic and not Ashkenazi was extremely slim.

Nevertheless, I made the eggs and was blown away by how cooking that dish made my whole house smell like my grandmother's apartment in Brooklyn (a borough in New York City). I started asking a new series of questions: what did my grandmother cook? What were her signature dishes? And I discovered that she made as many typical Sephardic recipes as she did Ashkenazi. Evidence of an African-Jewish background? Maybe. I'll never know for sure, but I do wonder.

Me? I have my dad's "Afro" hair underneath my White girl hair. It hides against my neck. It feels scratchy and breaks easily, and sometimes I just cut it all off, leaving odd holes hidden underneath my long gray mane. I took

89

my daughter to the salon a few weeks ago and watched the stylist cut her hair. She has the same wiry, kinky hair against her neck. And I felt proud to see it there, refusing to be soft and sweet, refusing to be ignored. She is part of me, and I am proud to pass on this confusing mess of ethnicity, religion and "race." She will make of it what she will, embracing all aspects of her past and creating an identity that, God willing, finds a world to inhabit that embraces her too.

After sixteen years working as a mental health professional, in 2012 Heather Rolland and her husband, Tom, embraced a drastic lifestyle change. Before long, she was splitting wood, rebuilding carburetors and baking bread. Famous for hiking every peak in the Catskill Mountains in a ballgown with as many as five rescued Malinois in tow, one dog in particular caught the eye of filmmaker Jessica Vecchione. The *Mica Movie* has opened to critical acclaim.

When Heather is not hiking, rescuing dogs and being a pioneer woman, you can find her creating custom jewelry for Malaprop Designs and writing. Her novels, *Bullbearpigdog; Finders, Seekers, Losers, Keepers;* and *Honey Melon Fudge* are available to buy on Amazon.

Heather's website: http://www.heatherrolland.com

Malaprop Designs: https://www.etsy.com/shop/MalapropDesigns

The Mica Movie: https://themicamovie.wordpress.com/

# A WOMAN'S JOURNEY IN THE COMPLEXITY OF OUR WORLD

Kim Suree Williamson—Australia

*Australian and Thai*

I remember the first time that I realised I was Asian.

I was just looking at the mirror one day, when I was a kid in primary school. I had a sudden realisation that I actually looked different to my friends. It was a revelation. Up to that point, it had never occurred to me to think about what anyone looked like or to notice any differences between us. It was exciting; I felt like I understood something that hadn't really been explained to me before. From then on, my awareness started to grow, and it started to shape my growing identity.

My dad is a White Australian from an average White family from Sydney; my mum is from Thailand with a generous sprinkling of Chinese ancestors, like many Thais. My dad is several generations Australian, dating back to White settlers, with some convict blood thrown in. His great-grandfather walked from Aberdeen to London with his little brother to join a sailing ship and had a scandalous career as a pirate. My mum's feisty grandma had a thriving teak wood business, a herd of elephants for the logging, a Chinese husband and a divorce.

My parents first met in Hawaii where they were both working. My dad was a surveyor, and my mum was a stunning surfer girl with long shiny hair and a master's degree. She used to cycle over to my dad's place to make him breakfast, picking mangos from the trees along the way. They fell head over heels in love and got engaged within three months. My dad wanted a white wedding in a church, surrounded by his family, and my mum's family in Thailand wasn't fussed, so they flew back to Australia to get married.

On their wedding day, my mum had a bouquet of daisies, a full-length  wedding gown and a wide, dazzling smile. She looked gorgeous. As she walked down the aisle holding her daisies, with a distant Thai family friend standing in for her dad and none of her friends in attendance, she told me that everyone's eyes were staring at her, like she was a bug.

For some of them, she was the first Asian person they had ever seen. She always told me, "Don't forget that no matter what anyone says, people will always treat you differently because you're Asian. Even if it's not to your face, people will always treat you like a second-class citizen."

However, I never understood what she was talking about. By the time I was growing up, Australia had embraced the waves of Italian and Greek immigrants, followed by the Chinese and Vietnamese and Lebanese, along with a mix of everything else. Very few of my friends at school had two parents who were born in Australia. I rarely experienced any form of racism—only when I travelled overseas, or occasionally in Australia with petrol station attendants or shopkeepers speaking to my mum, who still sounded like she was fresh off the boat despite decades of living in Australia.

Later at university, a lecturer made a point of how politically incorrect and intellectually lazy it is to lump all "Asians" into one category. Yet, when I was a kid growing up, being "Asian" was a strongly unifying identity. I had several friends whose parents were generically Asian; I never really knew where they were from—probably Malaysia, Hong Kong, Sri Lanka, China, Thailand, Indonesia, India and more—and it didn't matter. Our mums went to yum cha together; we had birthday parties with tables full of proper food, like fried rice and samosas, and all of us were forced to excel at our homework, among other cultural clichés.

It was pretty simple and lovely. I always felt Australian, because it was obvious that that's what being Australian meant.

I also remember the first time that I realised I wasn't Asian. I was eighteen, and I had taken a year off my university studies. On my mum's prompting, I decided to spend it living in Thailand. It was the first time that I had lived there by myself. I had never learnt to speak Thai as a kid since my mum didn't see the point: Australian society around the time I was born was strong on assimilation and light on encouraging diversity. So I moved to Bangkok, somewhat mute, and stayed in an apartment on Sukhumvit Road, right in the heart of the business and expat district.

I found that *nobody* thought I looked Asian.

Or at least, no one thought I looked Thai—sometimes I got Indonesian, or Indian or *any other* vaguely Asian country that was *not here*. That wasn't the only disparity. Having grown up with my Aussie girlfriends being jealous of my tanned skin through summer and through winter, people now unfailingly admired my white skin. In Australia, everyone thought I looked like my mother; in Thailand, everyone thought I looked like my father. And I discovered that people thought I looked *beautiful.* All the pop stars and movie stars and fashion models were of mixed blood, and I happened to fit the genetic make-up of the most striking people in the country. In Australia, I fitted the geeky, violin-toting, maths-studying stereotype; I looked like every other small Asian kid and never got much attention. In Thailand, people joked that I had won the Miss Universe competition and would star in soapies[12]. It was as baffling as it was flattering.

Not only that, but I realised that as a university student in Australia, I was poor. With my same scholarship in Thailand, I was *rich.* I could spend a lot more than many of my friends and still have money left over for overseas travel. The differences were more than just cultural—it was global economics laid bare. I soon learnt never to say enthusiastically to new friends, "Come visit me in Australia!"

I also found that people perceived me differently, depending on whom I was with. Living in Bangkok, my Thai girlfriends and I used to go out dancing. We all spoke English, we were young and we enjoyed dressing up and going out. My girlfriends all had quite dark skin, and when I was with them— especially in nightclubs—people would often treat us like we were lower class or even prostitutes. Not in a malicious way, but just as a reflection of the reality that the vast majority of girls who looked like us and behaved like us were prostitutes. This infuriated me. It rankled me how Thais, especially

---

[12] Soap operas

rich ones, would look down on me, never overtly, just in dismissive or disapproving looks. I was hyper-aware of how short my skirts went, how cheap my shoes looked and how bare my arms were. However, as soon as I opened my mouth and spoke English, and it was clear that I was not even able to speak Thai, it was like a switch was flicked. I was suddenly perceived to belong to the most desirable echelons of society—overseas educated, well off and *White*. It was striking and slightly disturbing. It showed me the malleability of our cultural and social cues that express status and our place in the social hierarchy. At the same time, it made a variety of identities available, fluid and interchangeable—without enforcing a need to choose.

A few years later, I spent a year on exchange to a Thai university. After all this time, I wanted to learn to speak Thai so badly, and I wanted to learn how to fit in. I wanted to be able to embody whatever I hadn't yet learnt how to do, to prove that I could hold this identity that I felt belonged to me, but had actually no clue about. My university supervisor—an elegant, ageing female professor of the Thai language—told me that the purpose of my exchange was to inculcate in me how to be a Thai woman, with all its accompanying principles, values and manners. It was a disaster.

I resented my fellow Thai university students, especially the girls with their tiny fake designer handbags, perfectly matte skin and deferential attitudes. My university supervisor made my lecturers stand me up in front of my classmates to criticise my hair for not being brushed (it was brushed, just not straightened), my shirt for not being ironed (it was ironed, just not ironed long enough) and for wearing pants instead of the standard skirt uniform. She forbade me from taking classes like scuba diving because she announced that it would distract me, so I took them anyway. I had meetings with her where she lectured me on the importance of pushing the chair back into the desk once I'd left, and I was furious she hadn't asked about my studies or whether I was *happy*.

95

She finally had a meltdown when I told her I was moving house without her permission. On my arrival to the town, she had found a place for me in a rather expensive apartment block with security guards and didn't support the idea of me renting my own place. I told her that I had never met any of my neighbours and that I wanted to be part of a normal community. I told her that one night I had left my door unlocked and had been gassed and robbed (just my phone, not my passport or my computer), and that my current neighbour was a girl whose routine involved loud sex with a variety of guys every night and throwing up violently every morning in her bathroom that shared an air vent with mine. My elderly supervisor insisted that I wasn't responsible enough to rent a house on my own, despite not having lived at home for almost ten years, because there were, god forbid, university students living on that street who did drugs and neighbours with toddlers and kittens. She argued that my poor language skills would lead to misunderstandings if I tried to communicate with them and that had to be avoided. Most of all, she said I had to listen to her because she was my elder, and I told her anyone would be stupid for following instructions if it was clearly terrible advice.

She contacted her Australian counterpart and tried to fail me on my exchange year. Luckily, I was acing all my actual subjects with my actual teachers.

At the age of thirty, I finally got a Thai passport, a Thai national ID card, and I got to invent a new signature for myself in Thai script. It was an emotional experience for my whole family, Thai and Australian. My journey of exploring identity and meaning has been lengthy; it's not straightforward and it's certainly not complete. These have been experiences of difference and belonging; of growing up not quite as part of the mainstream, but a great deal more than being an outsider. Not just different values, but multiple; not different perspectives, but manifold, often co-existing within contradictory frameworks. I think I crack Asian jokes a little more often, and I laugh at White jokes a little harder. I'm a little more aware, a little more empathetic, and maybe a little less committed to the universal truths of one group of people over another. In other words, through that openness and resilience, I am as well-equipped as I can be to embody a woman's journey in the complexity of our world today.

Kim Suree Williamson is half Thai and half Australian. She grew up mostly in Melbourne, Australia, but has lived in half a dozen countries around the world. She splits her time between Australia during the warmer months, and northern Thailand with her Thai family over the Melbourne winter.

Kim holds multiple degrees from one of the top universities in Australia. She is an editor, proofreader and writer specialising in academic and business writing.

# EAST MEETS WEST: WHERE DO I BELONG?

Sarah Ellingworth—England, United Kingdom

*English and Indian*

My father came to England from India in the early 1960s and my mother hailed from a large Catholic family in Manchester, England. I have always joked that you would find it hard to engineer a greater culture clash.

I have a brother ten months older and a non-identical twin sister. I am the only child to look in any way "non-English." I would describe myself as olive-skinned with very dark brown hair and brown eyes. My siblings both have blue eyes and fair skin; my twin sister even has blonde hair. My late mother always jokingly aligned our physical contrasts with dubious fathering—dustman[13] (brother), milkman (sister) and coalman (me).

---

[13] The term British people use for a garbage collector.

Considering this difference in physical appearance, our experiences growing up and even now are poles apart.

Young children can be very honest and direct. In Welwyn Garden City, where I spent my early years and went to primary school in the 1970s, there were no children of any colour. All my classmates were aware that my family was unusual and that I looked different. I was called a dazzlingly wide range of names that I understood to be unpleasant and unkind—Chocolate Drop, Sambo and Nig-Nog were the most common. Funnily enough, I think these names were directed at my brother and sister occasionally, but I bore the brunt of it. I remember a boy in Year 6 telling me he liked me but he could not associate with me, as my father was Indian. This was the most popular boy in the year and I don't remember being upset (I was probably just glad to have been a fleeting consideration).

I do remember wanting to look like a pretty, White English girl with fair skin, blonde hair and blue eyes. In the world I inhabited, these were the ultimate symbols of beauty; after all, this is what all our dolls looked like. Whether you had a Barbie or Sindy[14] doll—they both had the same attributes. Dark was not considered pretty, and all the messages I received as a primary-aged child reinforced that view.

Secondary school was much crueller. I went to a particularly tough secondary school. To give a barometer of how tough, anyone expelled in the locality ended up at my school, chairs and eggs were routinely thrown at teachers and bullying was open and widespread. The head of the youth wing of the National Front[15] went to my school. There were a few Indian boys in

---

[14] A popular British doll for young girls that was introduced in 1963. http://www.sindy.com/about-sindy/

[15] Founded in 1967, the National Front (NF) is a British far-right political party for Whites only. They are committed to repatriation. Despite denying they are fascist, they align themselves with neo-Nazis both in England and abroad. http://en.wikipedia.org/wiki/National_Front_(UK)

the years above me and none of them had a full set of front teeth. There was also a fair-skinned half-Black girl in my year. She was tall for her age, and she dealt with any hostility with great aplomb and, most effectively, by being stronger and louder than the children taking her on.

I was spat at and called names relentlessly. I learnt to keep my head down and not to stand out. I had left primary school confident and clever. Now no one wanted to be friends with me and I lost my confidence. I stayed focused on the clever.

I remember I had a physics teacher called Mr Singh. He was verbally abused by many of the children but seemed to deal with it really well. I don't think I saw him as a role model, but I did relate to him and I am sure he looked out for me in some small way as I always came top in his exams.

At fifteen or so I began to care less what others thought and began to form my own views on the world. I no longer wanted to dress the same as everyone else and began to see that my differences were something to be celebrated. I wonder if this would have been the same had I had ginger hair or teeth that stuck out? I guess for any features that make us different, at some point we learn to accept them, live with them and ultimately love them. I guess this is what we understand to be "growing up."

Meanwhile, at home, my physical difference to my siblings continued to cause much amusement to the Indian side of my family. I have never really considered whether I acted differently because of it until writing this essay and I am still not sure, but would not rule it out. Outside the family, I was an obvious target for cheap racial slurs and derogatory behaviour. Inside the family, my father was very fair-minded and treated us as equals. My mother came from more old-fashioned stock and, although she wanted me to do well at school, she was vocal about my brother's success being more important than my sister's or mine (this was definitely a red rag to a bull and not a view I cared to accept).

Looking more Indian also meant having more hair. Particularly on my upper lip. I remember being taunted at school for having a moustache, and this was something that developed into much more of an issue as I got older. Indian girls do have so much more hair, and facial hair can be really embarrassing. I used to dye the hair above my upper lip (with Jolen that never really worked) and also spent years rubbing it off with a hair-removal mitt. It grew back thicker and darker. As soon as I could afford it, I started paying for weekly electrolysis and over a six-month period, it was permanently removed. The best money I ever spent.

Into adulthood, my hair has become a huge asset. Most Indian hair is thick and strong, and I am lucky to benefit from it. And who knew that Indian skin aged so well? Approaching fifty, I have fewer lines and wrinkles than my contemporaries due to a higher elasticity in my skin—and I can thank my father for this too. I have also passed this on to my sons, whose father is English. Although they are fairer in colour than I am, both my boys have wonderfully thick, strong hair and darker-than-average skin with a gentle olive tone. I tell them this is their Indian heritage and they are very lucky. They agree with me and recognise these inherited assets. I did not feel the same at their age.

## Where Do I Belong?

It can be a challenge wondering where you belong and where you fit in. I certainly felt this growing up. I was made to feel different from other English people around me. But I also knew I didn't belong in India, where I felt like an alien. I first visited India when I was eleven years old. It was an amazing experience.

I went with my twin sister, and we were the centre of attention wherever we went. I expect this is because we didn't look Indian and, of course, my sister had blonde hair. My family were lovely and so welcoming. As children, we were fed all sorts of sweets, treats and goodies we never had back home—I ate so much sugar it made me ill. But the environment we moved around in was very strange, and the sight of lepers up close and seeing children being beaten in the streets, or begging and clearly hungry, really affected me.

I soon learned what "mother tongue" really meant—my father spoke Hindi, worked long hours and was unable to pass any language skills on to his children. Instead, my mother looked after us. If she had been the Indian parent there is a very high chance that my siblings and I would have been bilingual. Without Hindi language skills, trying to relate with my family, particularly my elders, was impossible. The communication barrier certainly added to my sense of not belonging.

My family in Delhi had a servant called Baddhu—apparently my sister and I really upset the equilibrium by hitting a balloon around one of the bedrooms with him. I think he should have been working and not fraternising with children who were from a higher caste. I don't know if he got into trouble, but I asked after him for a few years before finding out that he had run away. At eleven years old, Baddhu was my age and he did not have the freedom to play—he was a servant. I could not reconcile this then and cannot now.

To this day, my family in India use servants all the time—there will always be someone willing to work for next to nothing. Relatives are often shocked when they stay with us in England and see that my husband and I work, cook and run our household by ourselves. My cousin's jaw dropped on one visit when he saw my husband setting up the ironing board and iron. I recently taught one of my cousins to make a cup of tea. Back in Delhi, there are plenty to do that for him.

This leads me on to the position of women. As an undergraduate, I really began to understand how different lives were in the 1980s for women compared to men in India (this may still be the case now but to a much lesser extent). As an adult female, I had to eat with the women in the kitchen, and only

after the men had eaten all they wanted first. Not only did this mean that the food may have run out, but it was also cold by the time we were allowed to eat. Having been brought up with Western ideals, this was hard for me to accept. I also found the conversations sexist and I was just not used to that. I would ask a relative a question and he would direct the answer to the man standing next to me. I found this infuriating and I was quite indignant.

These cultural differences were stark and increased my sense of alienation—by the time I was eighteen, I loved being Indian and was proud of my heritage, but I felt like a foreigner when I visited. Now, while I feel lucky to not have just one culture but two, I know I could never live in India. I am thoroughly Westernised and could not adjust to such a different society. Still, I tell my boys they have two homes, and one of these is in New Delhi.

## Are the Stereotypes True?

My father definitely had the Indian work ethic. He was such a hard worker. It made time with him very special, as he was often busy working, running his own businesses. I hope this work ethic has passed on to me, and I definitely hope to pass it on to my children.

He also really valued education and wanted us to do well. As a result, my brother and I were the first in our family to go to university. Now my children jokingly call me a "tiger mother," but they know that I want them to be the best they can with the talents they have and try their hardest. This quiet expectation underpinned my childhood.

Another fundamental cornerstone of my Indian upbringing was to respect my elders. It may once have been a cornerstone of British cultural life, but I think this is waning. At my wedding sixteen years ago, we had guests attend from India, Canada and Germany (representing the respective groupings of my Indian family) and many from Leicestershire and other parts of the UK, including my husband's grandmother. She was ninety years old and in a wheelchair. Great Gran Alice was the ultimate matriarch of the family, and she was very old fashioned with her taste in food (pasta was considered "foreign"). We made allowances for her, as in her lengthy lifetime she had accommodated rather a lot of change.

Looking after Great Gran Alice appeared to be a chore for her Leicestershire family during the wedding celebrations. However, my young Indian cousins fought amongst themselves to push her wheelchair—they saw it as a great honour to look after the eldest family member. They treated her like royalty and catered for her every whim. To my utter amazement at the Indian buffet the following day, Great Gran Alice tucked into the curries like everyone else—she embraced my Indian relatives and a whole new type of cuisine.

I hope my children learn the value of respect for their elders too. Those who have gone before have wisdom and experience, which should be shared and cherished by younger generations.

Sarah Ellingworth is half White and half Indian and lives with her White husband and two sons in England. She is a practice manager for a local General Practitioner surgery centre.

# CHAMELEON

Jeremy Gelfand—United States

*Japanese and Russian Jewish*

I never really thought about being Biracial when I was growing up. I knew my father was Russian Jewish and my mother was Japanese. I thought nothing of it. I grew up on the Upper West Side of Manhattan (New York City) in a multi-cultural and multi-ethnic neighborhood with kids who came from all socio-economic backgrounds.

I knew plenty of other kids who were Biracial too: Black/White, Portuguese /White, Jewish/Puerto Rican, Italian/Haitian, Japanese/Dominican, and so on. I hung out with kids on 100th Street and Riverside Drive; I hung out with other kids on 101st Street and West End Avenue and I hung out with kids in the schoolyard on 96th Street (between West End and Riverside Drive).

I was a chameleon.

I could hang out with the "preppy" White kids or the "urban" Black and Puerto Rican kids. The common theme among these different groups of kids was that anyone could hang out as long as you weren't an asshole. Nobody cared what your nationality was. It didn't matter what your socio-economic background was. It just didn't matter.

Apart from meeting my mother's sister, her husband and their children, I never met my grandparents or any other relatives on my mother's side. We have distant relatives in Japan, but my mother didn't keep in contact with them. On my father's side, I met my grandmother and about twelve of her sisters and countless other cousins and so-called aunts and uncles.

My grandfather passed away before I was born, so I never met him. I know my grandmother and all my aunts and other relatives loved us, but I always felt like an outsider during family gatherings. I guess it's because my father didn't marry a nice Jewish girl like his parents wanted him to.

My grandmother didn't show the same affection to my mother like she did to my brother, my father and to me. As time passed, my paternal grandmother's side of the family got smaller. People started passing away and/or they started moving to warmer climates.

It seemed like my grandmother realized she had to accept my mother because we were the only family she had left. I wouldn't say my Jewish family was racist, but they were definitely prejudiced. I guess I can understand why because they immigrated to America to escape the Nazis, and they believed that you should stay with your own kind, especially in a new country, as did numerous other immigrants. Fortunately for my parents, they didn't share their parents' viewpoint.

My parents didn't raise my brother or me with Japanese or Jewish traditions. We were raised as typical American kids. We didn't celebrate Japanese or Jewish holidays. My mom introduced us to Japanese food growing up, but my brother and I weren't fond of it, so she didn't make it. To young kids, sushi was not appealing. Our grandmother introduced us to Jewish food, but my brother and I weren't very fond of it either, except for matzo ball soup, and we only really ate it whenever we went to her house to visit.

Looking back, I wish my parents would have introduced us to more of their families' culture and traditions, but I guess my parents saw themselves more as Americans than Japanese or Jewish.

Growing up, I was often mistaken for being Puerto Rican because I had some pigmentation to my skin. I didn't mind because I was always attracted to Puerto Rican and Black girls, so that made it easier for me to "rap" to them. I often thought if they knew I was White from the start, they might not have given me the same opportunity to talk to them.

It was easier for me to date Puerto Rican girls than Black girls. Even though it was the '80s, I guess I thought they wouldn't date a White guy because of the possible "backlash" they would get for dating outside their race. As I got older and as time passed, it seemed that interracial dating became less and less of an issue for me and the girls I dated—especially Black girls.

I joined the military in 1994 and again I was often mistaken for being Puerto Rican. I was actually stationed in Puerto Rico and people couldn't

believe I wasn't Puerto Rican. I would point to the name tag on my uniform and say, "Does Gelfand sound Puerto Rican to you?"

While stationed in Virginia, I met a beautiful Black woman, Chandra, and we were married in 2008. We lived outside of Richmond, Virginia. We often got curious looks from people—including Black people.

Black men at times were disrespectful to us. They would tell my wife she was a sell-out or they would tell me I couldn't handle her. We received the same treatment when we were stationed near Savannah, Georgia.

One of our neighbors was a military couple and one day they came by the house to welcome us, but my wife wasn't home. The wife was really nice to me until she finally met my wife. For some reason, she wasn't as friendly to me after that. The husband was still really nice to both of us. The funny thing is they, too, are a Biracial couple! He is White and she is Japanese!

As I stated in the beginning, growing up in New York, I never really thought about race. As I grew older, I guess I took more note of it. When questionnaires ask me to indicate race, I always put White and Asian, even though the instructions may say select only one. I always felt I was denying my mother's half of me if I only selected White.

When people ask me my heritage, I always say Russian and Japanese. The usual response is, "Really?" I always get, "I thought you were Hispanic or Italian." I'm proud of my multi-cultural background. I'm proud my parents raised me to accept people as they are.

Unfortunately, my mom passed away before I was married, but I know she would have accepted my wife with open arms. My father told me I "done good" when he met Chandra! Fortunately, my stepchildren see me as Dad and not as a "White stepfather." I'm lucky that my family doesn't see race either.

Jeremy Gelfand grew up in Manhattan's Upper West Side during the 1970s and 80s. His mother was Japanese and his father was Russian and Jewish. Following college, Jeremy worked in the private sector until 1994 when he enlisted in the United States Army.

Jeremy proudly served from August 31, 1994 until August 1, 2015, where he rose in rank to Master Sergeant with tours in Afghanistan, Iraq, Egypt, Kuwait, Germany and Korea.

Today, Jeremy lives in the nation's capital, working as a paralegal.

# BORN FROM A PARADOX

## Souad Yasmine—France

*Algerian and French*

Do you ever feel like you belong nowhere? I do, sometimes. Actually, I feel like I'm born from a paradox.

On 9, September 1962, after seven years, the Algerian War ended and a lot of stories began. Algeria became independent after more than a century of French colonisation, but the war left a huge wound in people's hearts and minds that has, still, a big impact today.

My name is Souad. I was born in Paris, the "City of Love," to a French mother and an Algerian father.

That's why I speak of a paradox. Being mixed with French and Algerian blood is really special to me in many ways. It can also be a little bit disturbing.

French/Algerian rap artist Médine put that into words perfectly in one of his songs. Loosely translated, he speaks of having mixed blood, being half colonist, half colonised. He explores his double identity, claiming he is a schizophrenic of humanity, and that old friends exist in his DNA[16].

And that's a perfect description of how I feel. As I was saying, this war left a huge wound in people's hearts. This is a really complex story because the subject has never been really tackled by the French government, and at the same time, Algerian people want the recognition of their pain, of the millions of people that were killed, tortured and more.

There is a real tension between France and Algeria. People with an Algerian background have a strong love for Algeria; they are proud to be from that ethnicity, proud of their ancestors that were tortured and killed for their country's freedom against the colonists. What is creating tension is that they live in the old colonist country now. There is a real love-hate relationship and politicians always seem to try to accentuate this phenomenon, even when they see Algerian flags flying at football games where they're not playing. They say that people have to choose. There's no real integration. For many French people, you have to reject your roots, your culture and your religion in order to be considered French.

That's why I'm talking about a paradox. It doesn't come only from the history of my ancestors, but also from the way that people look at me. I mean, to French people I'm an Arab, but for some Arabs, I'm a French girl. That really makes me feel weird, especially back when I was a teenager. I didn't know how to speak Arabic, my mum was French and I wasn't going to Algeria for my holidays. But I was feeling closer to my Algerian side and the fact that I was half-French made me believe that I had to justify myself and convince people that I was Algerian too.

That feeling went away with time.

---

[16] From the song "Alger pleure" by Médine: http://genius.com/Medine-alger-pleure-lyrics

But growing up brought another issue: religion. My mother comes from a Christian background while my father is a Muslim, but neither one is devout.

As a child, and then as a teenager, I never ate pork or drank alcohol. When I was still quite young, I felt closer to Islam, but never really practicing either. When I turned seventeen, eighteen and nineteen, and met the right people in my life, I learned more about my religion and started to practice it.

The more I tried to be a better Muslim by praying and learning, the more I felt lonely in my family. Fortunately, I was surrounded by amazing people, especially my best friend, who supported me and helped me gain confidence in my faith, my choices and become who I am today.

Religiously, I was always really quiet when I was in my mum's family. I didn't want to show them too much of my faith because being a Muslim is not really trendy in France, if you know what I mean. It's actually seen as a bad thing by many people there.

But on July 13, 2014, I decided that I couldn't hide it anymore. I wanted to wear the hijab, which is the headpiece that Muslim women wear to cover up their hair. It was a difficult choice to make since in France it's not tolerated at school or at work (with a few exceptions), but I felt that I was doing the right thing.

I have to admit that being Biracial has been, again, the source of many problems I've had after making that decision. Some people in my family rejected me or criticised me, saying that I was "dressing up as a Muslim but I was not one of them," or that I should be ashamed to do that to my mother or to my French grandmother.

It's actually really difficult to be confronted by discrimination in your own family where you're supposed to find your best allies. But it also made me stronger, making me realise that I should never stop being myself and doing what I want to do because I'm not doing anything other than just living my life in the way that I want to.

It's funny how being multiracial can be seen as a beautiful thing by some people until you reach some points that they dislike. After that, you have to follow the other side of your ethnicity or risk rejection. It's sad because it ruins the beauty of being multiracial, of having two or more cultures, of being physically different, of choosing your religion. Being multiracial can be seen as a wonderful gift.

Don't get me wrong—I may sound kind of negative, but I don't want to lie. Being multiracial has brought me problems that I wouldn't have if I had been only from one ethnicity. But at the same time, all of those problems make me proud of who I am. I'm proud to walk next to my blue-eyed mum, with my hijab on, looking like we have nothing in common when in fact we're everything to each other. I think it's a wonderful message against racism and Islamophobia.

But you know what? I want to believe that none of that actually matters. As cheesy as it sounds, we're all world citizens, we're free-minded people, and we should be proud of who we are. Being mixed race is a wealth, it opens your mind and it makes you more tolerant because you know by your own experience that sometimes it can be really difficult and tricky to please both sides of your family.

But what really matters is how we manage to accept each other, to respect ourselves in our choices, but also in our relationships with others. Never be ashamed to be different or to have issues with things that can be easy for other people. Let's just be ourselves—free, multiracial and proud.

Souad Yasmine is half French and half Algerian. She has a degree in Law and a master's degree in International Humanitarian Action. She lives in Paris, where she works as a translator.

# AN OPEN LETTER TO MY DAUGHTER

Erica Hayes—United States

*Mother of English, German, Korean
and Puerto Rican child*

D*ear Evangeline,*

*You'll be starting kindergarten this fall, a time that, for me, is both exciting and laced with trepidation. You've spent the first five years of your life with me or your father or another family member. But once September arrives, you'll be heading out into the world for a good chunk of time, without me or your father or any of those other family members.*

*Of course I want to believe that you will thrive, that you will love your teachers and your classmates and continue on your journey of discovering what excites you about life. I'd like to think your time at school will result in curiosities being sated and the roots of lifelong friendships being established. At kindergarten orientation, I watched as you easily interacted* with your peers. I watched how you listened attentively as the principal spoke, welcoming this incoming class of kindergartners. It was heartwarming. It was smile inducing. And yet, I could not help but notice that we were one of only a few other non-White people there.

Which got me thinking. Yes, things have changed significantly since I was a girl, but this area where I grew up, where you'll now grow up, is still mostly White people. I could not help but wonder if you realized this, though I tend to think not. Being adopted into a White family at a very young age, I was never aware that I was different until one of my first grade classmates asked if I was aware that my skin was the color of poop. And all of a sudden, it was as though a switch had been permanently turned on, that awareness had been brought to light. Sometimes, I suppose, ignorance really is bliss.

Throughout my school years, people assumed that I was good at math (I'm not), ate only pork-fried rice (I'm not Chinese), and would respond to "Kwan," "Wong" or "Lee." (Actually, I might respond to Lee, as it was my last name in Korea and now one of my middle names.) And even to this very day, in this town I grew up in, that way of thinking continues. I had to take some recycling to the dump and decided to stop by the free shop. A woman approached, holding a painting that had some vague black marks across the top.

"Excuse me," she said, "could you please tell me what this says?"

Clearly, it wasn't a language, but even if it was, I wouldn't be able to read it.

Shortly thereafter, another woman approached and asked if I knew the Wongs, from Sudbury, which is a town about a hundred miles from where we are.

So naturally, I wonder if these sorts of things will happen to you. Worry about it. Because I can handle it, and because I'm used to it and it doesn't make me feel bad. But then I realize what has been my experience will *probably not be yours. You don't look Asian. Or not entirely. You are half Asian, but you're also a quarter Puerto Rican and a quarter European mix. And so then my worry shifts: What is that going to mean for you?*

*Your father did not grow up in a predominately White area, but he found difficulty fitting in, nonetheless. He was too dark for the White kids, too light for the Hispanics, and, he didn't speak Spanish. Where do you go when no one will accept you for who you are? Who do you identify with?*

*So I wonder how you are going to fare in this world. Some people believe that half-Asian women are the most beautiful in the world. I have seen the advantages beauty can afford a woman, but I also know the way it can affect her, being judged solely on looks. From the day you were born, people have commented on your beauty, but it is seldom without also including the word "exotic". I don't want your life to be unnecessarily difficult, of course, but I want people to see you for who you are—for the things you do, for what you like. You are a sweet, funny, goofy girl with a quirky side she isn't afraid to show.*

*What sorts of notions will people have about you? Will you constantly be plagued with questions about your ethnicity? I know how tiresome that can be. I may only be one race, but people are constantly asking, trying to guess and usually guessing wrong. People, strangers, have come up to your*

*father and hazarded a guess about his ethnicity, as if they were contestants on a game show, hoping to finally come up with the right answer.*

*"Italian?"*
*"Portuguese?"*
*"Hawaiian?"*
*"Arabic?"*
*"Chilean?"*

*I do not believe, in the thousands of times people have approached him, that anyone has ever guessed correctly.*

And will it be disconcerting that there don't seem to be any people who really look like you? Your eyes are larger than mine but not as large as your father's. I have straight hair, your father has curls; yours is somewhere in between—thick, wavy, and gorgeous, dark but shot through with caramel and auburn colored highlights. The sort of hair I have always coveted. Your skin tone is less gold than mine, less olive than your father's.

*I've heard many times that the best breed of dog to get is a mixed breed; they are the strongest, the healthiest, the most vibrant. I'd like to think the same is true for people, and that, if anything, this mixing of heritages will be an asset to you and your brother as you go through life.*

*But I know I won't always be there to help you field the questions that come your way, questions that might be asked out of simple curiosity or ignorant maliciousness. Times have changed since I was your age, progress has been made, but I still know that you will be in the minority when you start kindergarten this year. Above all else, I want you to be comfortable with the skin you're in. I want you to have an unshakable faith in yourself, in your abilities, in all the things that don't matter when it comes to the color of your skin. I hope that you can find the balance to appreciate your heritage, your unique background, yet not let it be the one thing that defines you, either in your eyes or the eyes of those around you. Because we are more than how we look, we are more than these physical bodies that we are inhabiting during this lifetime. I know from my own experience that the world is not color blind; I hope your experience can be one in a world that is color appreciative.*

*With much love and admiration,*
*Your mom*

Erica Hayes was born in Seoul, Korea, and came to the United States when she was nine months old. She grew up on Cape Cod, lived in San Francisco for a decade, and returned to the Cape after her two children were born. Her children are Korean, Puerto Rican, English and German. She lives with her husband, two children and two stepsons on Cape Cod, where she works at a bike shop and as a freelance writer. When she's not working or hanging out with her family, she's most likely off riding her mountain bike somewhere she'd never be able to get to on foot.

# ONE OF THE TRIBELESS

## Chance Maree—United States

*Cherokee, Italian, Scottish and German*

Instead of being born with an angel perched on one shoulder and a devil on the other, my father handed over a conscience from the Cherokee/Italian nation while my mother installed her own advocate from good German/Scottish stock. If asked to choose a familial alliance or to identify my heritage, I would say that I've sided with none of the above. I know the neutrality of my position sounds odd and requires some explanation.

Growing up, I was exposed to both families. Visits to my Cherokee/Italian relatives were exhausting hours filled with loud conversations, boisterous laughter, unnecessary yelling and wild tales of physical clashes, some of which involved the police. My grandmother was from the Ohio clan of the Cherokee Nation. She was very short with high cheekbones and gray eyes—we believe she may have had some Irish in her bloodlines. Although I'm tall with brown eyes, I have her cheekbones.

Indian history attracts and saddens me. I've researched their tragic stories and visited sacred sites. Perhaps my Cherokee blood led me to my vision quest in the Mexican desert, which I wrote about in my first novel. In my third novel, my characters are mixed-breed Comanche, and the story takes place along Devil's Backbone, an area of Texas where Indians and settlers clashed. The Indian threads in my stories developed organically, rather than rising from a conscious theme. Genes make appearances in odd ways.

Grandmother claimed her ancestors mixed with immigrants who worked and traded along the Cincinnati River. She herself married a Sicilian immigrant; he was the calm one in the family. Grandfather worked in a paint factory; at some point they opened a restaurant/bar. Together they had nine children. I believe each of my father's sisters went on to have nine children as well. By the time I arrived, it was a large group who loved to gather everyone together for holidays.

During those events, there was plenty of boasting—so-and-so girl relative had to be carried away from a screaming match before it turned into a fight, while the boys' tales went directly to the combat, intermingled with drunken binges, illicit affairs, pregnancies, high jinks and paybacks, each of which empathized a motivation that supposedly stemmed from some positive trait such as loyalty, bravery, or a fierce demonstration of love. Unlike most of the children at these gatherings, my eyes never sparkled as these tales were spun, and I never had narratives of my own to offer.

Visits to the German/Scottish affairs were rare and less crowded. The adults stayed in the main house, while we children played with toys or helped ourselves to the tomatoes and strawberries growing in well-tended gardens. I never learned many of the names of those relatives, except for the nice white-haired woman who gave me an antique statue of a donkey pulling a cart. She patted me on the head and told me to call her Aunt Honey. I later learned that she was the sister of my grandmother. I remember once, after a birthday celebration, my mother drove us home because my father was drunk. He never drank that much at his own family parties. I believe mother would have liked more frequent visits to her relatives, but secret adult undercurrents kept us apart.

Being a shy, reserved child, you might think I'd prefer the German/Scottish clan. The trouble is, I saw strengths and faults with both. While the Cherokee/Italians often exhibited poor judgment and a lack of focus, decorum and discipline, I appreciated their vitality, camaraderie and devotion to the idea of family. They loved drama, a life lived fully and, right or wrong, with all emotions displayed proudly up and down both their sleeves.

With the German/Scottish clan, the mood was calm and dignified, but you never knew what really was going on or where you stood. I was in my twenties before I learned of the decade when my grandmother and my father could barely stand one another, or that my grandmother was ostracized because she was twice divorced. Everything was secret and subdued. Perhaps my exposure to them taught me to observe people closely and imagine unstated meanings and motivations—a necessary skill for a novelist.

One of their most prominent traits was a fierce and stubborn independence. I had to enlist allies to convince my grandmother that she needed to travel from Ohio to Washington, D.C. for my wedding—she couldn't understand why I needed her there. Years later, her sudden death came as a shock to everyone, until they discovered that she had never filled prescriptions for heart medication given by her doctor. Her will and affairs were in perfect order. My grandmother had tidied up everything in preparation for her death, which came quickly, quietly and without drama.

Having been imprinted by both influences, I've had to accept the strengths and weaknesses of each. This tends to both soften criticism and temper pride.

During my college years, I investigated a variety of races, religions and cultures. While I had preferences in details such as ritual conduct and aesthetics, a voice coming from one or the other of my shoulders was always ready to squash any rise of personal bigotry.

To appreciate a complex subject such as heritage, I favor an objective perspective: Each person's tribe should be respected. Relying on stereotypes is not helpful. In fact, the archetypes of my two families could have been reversed; boisterous German/Scots and introspective Cherokee/Italians certainly exist. More important was the diversity itself, which affected my character and approach to life.

While I tend to focus on the positive aspects of my upbringing, there have been times when I've noted several disadvantages of living outside a tribe. For example, I notice that people who identify with a heritage or community are generally not as conflicted or analytical as I tend to be. I imagine that living under a group's influence provides fertile ground for certainty. Members of a tribe may be less tormented over what to think or believe, no need to achieve peace or balance in conflicts. They know which team to cheer for, whereas, even with something as innocuous as sports, I have never felt the passion of rooting for one team over the other.

During those exploratory college years, I hitched my mind to one religious cult after another. Ever the observer, I saw strengths and weaknesses from ideological tribes as well as genetic ones. By my late twenties, I withdrew from their influence as well. I follow my own path, which causes most of my religious friends to declare me a lost cause.

In complex arenas such as world politics, the need for separateness or distinction (whether between tribes or between individuals) appears to foster a feeling of superiority. This has many ugly implications in society. For one to be superior, another must be held inferior, and life is hard when people feel another tribe's boot upon their necks. The only prejudices I allow myself are those against people or cultures that are cruel, either to humans or animals. For that, I cannot accept rationalization or excuse. If the practice is one of tradition, I still will not hide my objection and disgust. And yes, I experience the sense of superiority of that conviction. It is a flaw that I wish could be remedied by any means besides complacency.

My Cherokee/Italian relatives were conscious of their lower economic status and the history of prejudice against those of their heritage. They were proud of me; I was the first of their family to go to college. Their poverty and lack of education doomed most of them to hard and dangerous labor, the physical and mental stress of which aged their bodies well before their times.

Of the two families, however, these folks would have welcomed me into their camp under any circumstance. In contrast, as of this day, since the death of my grandma and one uncle, I have no idea as to the whereabouts of any member of my middle-class German/Scottish family. Due to this, I refuse to attach value or integrity to a person as a factor of their education or bank account.

The Cherokee/Italian family told stories of discrimination that stirred intense emotion, peppered with rage and laughter, that somehow gave the family strength. My only personal brush with prejudice was during a job interview in Washington, D.C. with an African American manager whom I felt hated me on sight. Her questions and body language throughout the interview left no room for doubt the job could never be mine. Even then, I was an objective observer to her bias. Finally, I had a whiff in that one tiny moment of the daily experience endured by my African American friends.

If I had lived with discrimination, my feelings would have hardened, of that I'm certain. Once, while I worked as a technology professional in D.C., I rode in a car with three of my colleagues. We were all dressed in business suits. The car was quite nice; it belonged to an African American gentleman who was driving. When we stopped at a traffic light, a policeman pulled up beside us. I, in the passenger seat, and my two colleagues in the back seat, all turned to look at the officer who appeared to be staring into our car. My friend, who was driving, continued to look straight ahead. I noticed his face was hard-set, as though made of stone. Once the police car pulled away, my friend explained, "If you all hadn't been here, he would have pulled me over." I learned also of other African Americans, college-educated, corporate professionals, being stopped by police outside their own homes. They were constantly being asked, "What is your business here?" The stories made me angry and opened my eyes to how different lives can be for people of different races living in the same country, or even the same neighborhood.

My minority friends taught me what life is like growing up and raising a family in a country that appears to have disparate sets of laws based on skin color or economic standing. This, more than my own heritage, has shaped my world view. The difference we humans set among ourselves is fascinating, heartbreaking and mind-boggling, especially given that the similarity of DNA between a man and a chimp can be as high as 99.6%. Imagine how small the difference is between individuals or races.

Someday, as people continue to mix and intermarry, race will be a non-issue. Then, we will have to find other reasons to distance ourselves from others. Or perhaps we will all just learn to live in peace.

Chance Maree is Cherokee, Italian, Scottish and German and is a bootstrap novelist and story-telling enthusiast who gravitates towards upmarket fiction with a speculative slant. She has published three novels so far: *Alexios, Before Dying; Undazzled;* and *Dark Matter Tiding.* Chance has been transplanted to Texas by her astrophysicist husband where they live with three dogs and a native Texan, scorpion-killing cat.

For more information on Chance visit: http://ChanceMaree.com

# THE ECHO OF THE BIG MULTIRACIAL PACKAGE

### Lea Borinan Bernus—Spain

*Caribbean Black, Native American, French,*
*Tunisian and Russian*

Being born with a gazillion very different ethnicities has never been much of a headache and yet, it has always profoundly impacted my life whether I wished it to or not. My origins cannot be stamped on me; they are not obvious and still they can be guessed. They are an inherent part of me, playing a crucial role on my growing person, bringing to me traditions and values that nowadays tend to be forgotten.

My identity struggle started when I became a teenager. Soon after, I understood that people's invasiveness, curiosity and rejection of me were just the reflection of my own rejection of self. I did not know or accept who I was. But in order to accept my cultural and genetic heritage, I first had to understand it.

I was born in 1990 in Paris. Who knew that twenty years later, most people would be surprised about where I was born and what my nationality is.

BEING BIRACIAL ♂+♀=? where our secret worlds collide

I am French and so are my parents. My maternal grandparents technically are French too, from the Caribbean though. As for my father, his parents were Tunisian and Russian. Sadly, I have never had a chance to meet them or to know more about their life, and still my genome carries theirs. My inherited physical traits and my inextinguishable curiosity about Tunisia and Russia are embedded in me.

My mother raised me by herself. Shortly after my birth, we moved to Spain. I grew up in the constantly sunbathed Mediterranean beaches with much room for freedom. I always sought companionship without caring for color, nationality or even language barriers and it worked like a charm. I had many friends!

At that time, even if we lived in places where there didn't seem to be many people looking like us, life happened peacefully and lightheartedly— there were good times, times where identity questions didn't spring up and the word acceptance was in order.

My mother didn't raise me in a Caribbean way. I don't think she's ever felt very close to it, even if she knows more about Guadeloupe (an island in the Caribbean) than I do. She raised me in a way that would let me explore everything that my curiosity directed me to, with very little control over it. I was free to develop myself without opposition.

As for my grandmother, she grew up in Guadeloupe. She was brought up in a very traditional way; her mother was a teacher, and her father was a sailor and a musician. Tragically, he died at a very young age, and she was left to take care of her brothers and her sister while her strict mother raised them according to the local values and a strong Christian faith. My mother and her sisters were raised in a similar fashion and, as soon as she had a chance, she flew the nest to live without the oppression brought by my grandmother's traditions. Interestingly, my grandmother is mixed as well. So are my mother and my aunts. A mix of a mix.

Looking past our differences, we have kept our little family very close. My grandmother told me many things about her past and her education, and I can comprehend a few of the somewhat weird reactions that she has toward the modern world. She sees herself as a Black woman, or should I say Black *and* a woman. She also has an incredibly strong sense of social class as she grew up in a time when Caribbean society was still completely divided by money, social status and skin tones.

She's always been very keen on sharing our culture and history, and wants us to know where we come from. "Okay, we are French but not only that; we happen to have a rich heritage that deserves to be known, cherished and shared."

I feel like our perceptions of the world are very different. For me, being mixed race never really posed a problem. I was born in a time of acceptance. The big fights for racial rights had been fought and won, eventually becoming part of our history. That to me is the history before a fairer world between people from different races. Not that it's perfect on the matter, but it's a far cry from what it used to be fifty years ago.

My problem was different, in trying to put together all of those identities into my own. Making them a part of me, to be a more understanding version of myself and to grow stronger and more confident in the process. It happened over time and it develops still, thanks to my family, my friends and my own devouring curiosity.

In my family, we have never been big on being part of a community that shared origins with us. I guess that if we had, we would have needed a Caribbean, a French and an American Indian community at the same time, and that would be just on my mother's side.

I guess the idea of adding to the mix Russian and Tunisian makes it even more of a challenge!

Even though I didn't know my father or my extended family very well, I appreciate the cultural background they have left me. I am getting to know it by my own means, and it's always with a sense of wonder that I recognize two very different cultures that somehow just make sense to me as a whole.

I have traveled and lived in many different places. As my North African traits are fairly visible, people have often thought that I was from a Maghreb country and have started speaking to me in a language that didn't ring any bells. But I can't deny that if they recognized something that lets them have a certain familiarity with me, it had to be good.

In my early adulthood, I came back to live in Paris for a while and out of that ethnic recognition, I made a few mates from Morocco and Tunisia, learned more about their culture and much about myself as well. Somehow I could feel an echo. I was attracted to a reality that I'd never experienced and learning from their traditions felt completely natural.

No matter where I lived—France, Germany, Spain, Ireland or England— even in the most secular villages, I have always been welcomed. Maybe it's different elsewhere. I sometimes read very different stories from mixed people and that's normal; we all come from different backgrounds and environments. As far as mine goes, I have only on very rare occasion felt some kind of negative response toward my mixture.

I was born with that particular big cultural package and I consider myself very lucky. I have won a lottery that I have never even played! It might get confusing every now and then, but I always make sure to remember that everything in the universe originated from chaos.

At home with my mother, we speak French, English and Spanish, we share Caribbean, American Indian and French blood, and on my side Russian and Tunisian, too. Our culture is a European mix with strong ties from our family's varied cultures from the American, Asian and the African continents. We are proud of who we are, of our many different origins. We

keep on learning and sharing our cultural heritage, the same way it was shared with us.

And right now? I'm considering learning Russian and Caribbean Creole, which would make it easier to speak with some relatives. A trip to Russia too, in the summertime. I wonder if anyone will ever believe that I have Russian origins when I get there?

Lea Borinan Bernus is a translator and she writes in English, French and Spanish. She promotes natural health and, in her words, "has done a bit of everything." Her main writing platform is Natur'Choko:

http://naturchoko.com/a-journey-back-to-mother-nature/

# A MOTHER'S EPIPHANY

## Amy Myers—United States

*White, Mother of two White and Black children*

I remember vividly the day I realized what I was up against as the parent of a mixed-race child. Up until that day—that very profound and defining moment—I was simply the mother of an adorable, curly-haired, bubbly little boy.

Parenting has its challenges in general, and because I was a single mother, perhaps I just hadn't had the time to really think about the fact that my son was also half Black. Sure, I had seen "the looks" that some people gave in public; but for the most part, people adored this chubby little bronze-skinned baby with his gorgeous curly hair and fat little fingers and toes.

Until that day.

It was a gloomy fall day. It had been sprinkling rain off and on all morning, so I decided to take Kamron to McDonald's for lunch. He loved the play area, and I could sit and watch him while working on my homework; multitasking is a necessary skill for single mothers. I watched my toddler jump around and climb without a care in the world, as he had done many times before in this very same play area.

Observing him out of the corner of my eye, while half skimming/half reading some boring college textbook, I noticed him walking up to a much older boy, around nine or ten, interacting briefly and then walking away. He did this three different times, so I put my book down and walked over there. I don't remember feeling concerned at all, but more curious as to what was being said.

Just as I approached, I heard the older boy say, "No, go around. I told you, only White people are allowed on this slide."

Huh? Did I hear that correctly? No. He must have said something else...this is the twenty-first century after all...nobody behaves that way.

I decided to give the kid the benefit of the doubt. I called out and motioned for him to come over by me so I could ask him about what he had said. He looked confused, sort of glanced around, but then slowly made his way toward me.

"That's my son right there...the one you were just talking to. He's only two, so he probably doesn't understand what you are asking him to do. What did you say? Did you tell him he can't go on that slide?"

He looked uncomfortable, but he nodded slowly, his gaze never leaving my eyes. I was an education major in college, and I immediately considered this a teachable moment; an opportunity to help this boy understand why what he had said was inappropriate.

Apparently, I had overstepped my boundaries. Just as I was calmly telling the boy that the slides are for everyone, and it's not fair to exclude someone just because he or she is different, I saw, out of the corner of my eye, a blur. I turned just as a very large woman was bounding towards me, barely stopping six inches from my face.

Uh-oh...momma bear.

Her finger was in my face and her voice was elevated. "Don't YOU discipline MY son! If you have something to say to him, you find out who his parent is and discuss it with them."

At this point, everything seemed to fade out around me. All of the noises and movement that had surrounded me before seemed to disappear, and all I saw was this woman who was invading my personal space and breathing her hot Big Mac breath in my face. I lost it.

"Do you know what your son was saying to my son? Your son told my son that he couldn't slide on that slide because he isn't White." *There. That should shut her up. Now she knows her son is a bigot.*

What hadn't dawned on me—in my twenty-six-year-old naïveté—was that racism is a learned behavior. It hadn't even occurred to me that this young boy, who was full of hate and discrimination, had been molded by adults who were also full of hate and discrimination. It was so out of my realm of understanding because I had been raised in a household that was loving and accepting and respectful of others.

"Well, maybe if there wasn't trash like YOU in this world, he wouldn't have to worry about that, would he?" was her response.

Immediately I could feel the blood rising from my feet to the top of my head. I felt my fingers tingle, my armpits become damp and my ears heat up. I have never felt so much anger toward a stranger in my life.

At that moment, I hated that woman for so many reasons. I hated her for her ignorance, for her beliefs, but I mainly hated her for teaching that ugliness to her children, who would grow up in a world with my child and others like him, spreading racism and hate along the way.

That was the moment it really hit me.

My child isn't going to grow up like I did. He doesn't have the luxury of walking into a room and being treated as an equal. He will be in classrooms, on teams, in groups and at work with people who feel exactly the way these people feel about him.

Right now he is young and innocent and clueless to what is going on, but one day he will understand, and he is going to know that simply because of the way he looks, he is not accepted by all.

Somehow, between these jumbled thoughts and the physical manifestation of raw anger in my body, I managed to say something. It wasn't pretty. I unleashed on her, attacking her person briefly.

It was only briefly because I glanced over her shoulder, and there was her son. He looked terrified. He had tears in his eyes, and I could tell he was confused at all of the commotion.

At that moment it hit me that he wasn't the only child watching; the room was full of children, including my own who must have been terrified as well. I stopped screaming at my newfound nemesis, and I took a deep breath, gathered myself and said, "I feel sorry for you."

I turned around and located my son, grabbed his coat, and we headed out the side door. I didn't look back, so I don't know what she was saying or doing at that point. All I know is that I wanted to get out to my car as quickly as I could.

Luckily, my son was oblivious to what had happened, as most two-year-olds would be. The minute I sat in the driver's seat of my car, I began to sob. It was that deep "can't catch your breath" type of sobbing, the kind that makes you feel like you are five years old again and just found out that you can't actually marry your parents one day!

When my little episode was over, I looked in the rearview mirror at my son, who was staring at me with a look of utter confusion. "Okay, mommy?" he asked.

"Yeah, buddy. Mommy's okay. You okay?" "Yep. I okay," he said with a huge smile. My heart ached because I knew that I wouldn't always be there to protect him the way I just had. One day, he would have to face the little boy in McDonald's on his own, and that broke my heart.

Sixteen years have passed since that rainy day at McDonald's. I now have two mixed-race sons, and we have encountered more ignorant people and had to learn more life lessons along the way. People amaze me with their beliefs sometimes, but for every ignorant person who has crossed our path, we have met many wonderful, loving people who reaffirm my belief that things are getting better. I know my boys will always be viewed as "less than" by some people, but the truth is, it builds character and makes them stronger people.

I have always told my boys to hold their heads high and be proud of who they are. If someone can't accept them, they need to move on, because that person doesn't deserve to be in their lives in any capacity.

As for me being the parent of mixed-race children, I wouldn't change that for anything. I am so much more aware and open-minded as a person and a teacher.

I love all of my students, but there is a special place in my heart for children who are different, those who get left out or mistreated by others. I know that it takes a strong person to go through life feeling different from herself, and I am proud to say I have raised two very strong and confident young men.

Amy Myers is a single White mother of two Biracial boys living in Boise, Idaho. She is a high school English teacher with an MA in Literacy instruction. She loves to write.

# PIONEERS

## Yacob Cajee—England, United Kingdom

*South African, Indian, Bantu, Mauritian, Scottish and French*

G rowing up in a poor but cosmopolitan part of Coventry, just a long punt from Highfield Road football ground, the only race I was really aware of was the Grand National[17].

Even when I asked a man walking past my house what the football score was and he replied with, "Get out of my way, you little Black bastard," it didn't occur to my six-year-old brain that he or anyone else had a problem with my skin colour. Indeed, it took me another twenty years to process the significance of that moment to my mental, emotional and social development.

Both of my parents were from South Africa, my father's family from a small fishing village on the West coast of India. My maternal grandfather was also of Indian origin, via Mauritius (it's only in the last decade that I've

---

[17] Annual British horserace

discovered his grandmother was from Paris), so my complexion, hair and features mark me down as being Asian rather than African.

However, my mum's mum, with whom I spent many of my formative years, was a "Cape Coloured," a native South African of mixed White (Scottish) and African (Bantu) parentage. This helped explain the range of skin colours enjoyed by my mum and her siblings. Whilst she had the look of a pale-skinned Indian and her sister the olive skin and fine features of a Greek or Italian, one of her four surviving brothers was "black as the ace of spades," while another had such pale skin and ginger hair that he often passed himself off as White and would avoid sitting next to my dad on the bus home from work in 1950s London.

In the early days of employment monitoring, there were only six categories listed: White UK (have you noticed how White is always first?), White Irish, White European, Black, Asian and Other. It always amused me that I could tick five out of six boxes.

Nowadays it's still as difficult—am I Black/British, Asian/British or Mixed? And if I'm Mixed, am I African/Asian or Other (please specify)? I generally go for Mixed Other: British-born of African/Indian/Scottish/French ancestry, although I sometimes throw in Mauritian for good measure. The one great advantage this gives me is during sporting events, especially the cricket and rugby world cups, when I can claim allegiance to whoever happens to be winning—England, South Africa, India, Scotland or France.

I've had many a debate with people who tell me I'm not Black—there are many Asians who recoil with horror from the suggestion that they might be labelled as such, insisting that I am brown. What their prejudice reveals is a total lack of understanding of the political nature of the word Black rather than it being a description of colour.

In the same way, the White population is not actually white—in the words of E.M. Forster, they are, rather, "pinko-grey." By the same token, I am Black, not because of African heritage, and certainly not because of my skin colour in the way my Uncle Cass was Black. I am Black because of a shared cultural and political experience that excludes me and anyone else— be they African-Caribbean, Sri Lankan, Chinese or Malaysian—from the club that is White.

As a trade union activist in the 1980s, I was involved in establishing Black members' groups. Many were the occasions I argued with fellow Black members during those early days about the eligibility criteria for fellow trade unionists to join our group.

Many of my colleagues of mixed heritage had to fight long and hard for acceptance because their pale skins, it was suggested, protected them from the effects of racism. I argued that not only should the children of mixed-race partnerships be welcomed, but also the partners and parents (including adoptive parents) of anyone who identified themselves as Black.

I've experienced all sorts of racism down the years, abuse and physical violence at school and in the street, being overlooked for jobs, and even being sacked by Capita as a result of racial discrimination and pressure to discriminate.

In these post-Lawrence[18] days, it's rare that I experience open racism. Being called a Wog, Paki, Coon or Nigger is generally a thing of the past, although occasionally I'm still taken

---

[18] http://www.bbc.co.uk/news/uk-26465916 (Stephen)

aback by being told I should go back where I came from. People also still confuse me with the person who served them a curry on Saturday night or with the only other (much taller, much stockier) Asian member of the local golf club.

On the other hand, my wife, who is White, is still regularly regaled with open hostility to the Black and Asian community by those who don't realise that she is one of those "Paki-lovers" they so despise.

Out shopping one day near our home in Devon, she noticed the (ironically) Black Country accent of one of the shop assistants. Being from the Midlands herself, she began a conversation with the assistant—whereabouts was she from? How long had she been down here? The reply came back that she and her husband had moved down several years previously because "it was getting too dark, if you know what I mean."

Very recently, my wife was at an event where an acquaintance was telling a group of people about her daughter's new Labrador puppy. When someone asked what the dog was called, this woman thought it highly amusing to announce, "Whoopi—because she's a Black bitch!"

Perhaps, though, the most distressing experience for my wife came within a few weeks of our first child being born. When he was a few weeks old, she took him to the post-natal clinic where he was customarily weighed. When he registered slightly below the standard weight range for his age, the community midwife simply pronounced, "It's quite common for the children of immigrants to be malnourished." She took no account of the fact that my son was small at birth, nor was she interested enough to find out that I was born in this country's capital city. All that mattered was that my wife had taken this strange-sounding surname, which the midwife took as her licence to voice her prejudices about immigrants and their offspring.

Despite all the prejudice and discrimination we have experienced as a family, despite the impact on my career and the bullying and abuse my children experienced in school, we are all rightly proud of our mixed heritage, proud to be in the vanguard of what will become the norm in the increasingly integrated world in which we live.

Yacob Cajee was born in London of South African parents, with Indian, Mauritian, African, Scottish and French ancestors. Raised in the Midlands, Yacob studied English Literature at the University of London before beginning a career in public sector financial management. This has taken him across the length and breadth of England and he recently relocated to Pembrokeshire.

Yacob has been involved in equalities work for thirty years, helping to establish trade union Black Workers' Groups, securing fair holiday entitlements for part-time workers and writing the TUC guide to appropriate language in the workplace, *Diversity in Diction, Equality in Action*. As well as being a qualified accountant, Yacob is a registered hypnotherapist and massage therapist, and a freelance writer and editor.

# MAKEOVERS

## Mary Kay McBrayer—United States

*Lebanese, Hispanic, Scottish, Irish and Native American*

In the autumn of sixth grade, I developed a crush on a classmate whose first language was Spanish, but he almost always spoke English. Juan was in all my honors classes. He played a lot of Pokémon cards, knew all the words to "Bohemian Rhapsody" and he thought "boy bands" were stupid. Because I was an only child, I told my mother everything he did or said to me. After a month or so I grew impatient. I asked her for a makeover. I was an ideal candidate: a total nerd whose athletic father and exotic mother won her Most Attractive in the same small town Georgia high school. I deserved to be a late bloomer.

"Yallah," she said, "You're already beautiful. *Chou baddee?*"

"You have to say that because you're my mama," I replied.

She stood and walked me into her Victorian bathroom. I sat on the toilet lid where she pointed. My mother was never so naïve to believe looks don't matter. And she was never cruel enough to let me believe it either. She pulled a powdery black makeup bag from under the sink. When I asked if we could do the makeover in front of the vanity mirror like a real teen movie, she cut me off. "Light's better in here. You want my help, don't you?"

She plucked my eyebrows and my eyes streamed with tears, but I knew better than to complain. My brow bones had deep tan lines from late summer pool days, which she covered with matte powder. I blinked into her mascara wand. "You don't need eyeliner," she said.

"Just do it, mama. Do all of it, please."

She backed away, sliding pencils and creams into her bag. I leaned into the mirror. The counter pressed into my baby fat. Staring back at me over unused perfume bottles were Cleopatra eyes that should not have belonged to a twelve-year-old girl.

I was not pretty like my friends with their glittery eye shadows, sticky lip glosses and those two strands of fine hair falling middle-parted from their foreheads. My closest comparisons were Jasmine with the red suit and high ponytail seducing Jafar. Shakira belly dancing and staring into the camera before she bleached her hair. Anak-su-namun self-eviscerating rather than prostituting herself.

None of them were of my heritage exactly, but they were close enough and they were who I saw when I looked my reflection in the face.

My classmates noticed my makeover. My braids were untethered. A toothed headband pinned my mane off my face. My eyes seemed a little more open, a little wider set. Juan didn't talk to me any more or less than usual. Fifteen was too old for a first kiss, but I was determined. I came to school sophomore year with khakis and straight black waxy hair. I could run my fingers through it. My friends loved it, said I looked older and said they didn't even recognize me.

My high school sweetheart used to wait in the gym to walk me to trigonometry every day. One day it rained, which meant my hair wasn't going to stay straight. He grinned and said he liked my hair curly best. "It looks good both ways, I mean," he backpedaled, "but I like it that way. It looks natural. It's exotic."

I ran my hand up his forearm.

I liked it best this way too.

His friend propped beside him, looking down onto the basketball court at one of my boyfriend's teammates. He said, "Did you hear who he's dating now?"

We nodded.

"That interracial dating is so gross," he said.

My boyfriend and I said nothing. He finally kissed me on my mother's wraparound porch in the wooden swing. It took him months. We sat out there till dark. When my mom flipped the lights to tell me to come in, he cranked up his F150 and went home.

We dated for a while and then he graduated. We gradually forgot about each other, and boy after boy whom I dated either never brought up that we were of different ethnicities, or they mentioned it gracelessly. I don't know if there is a graceful way to ask those questions about race, but it's foolish to pretend they don't exist. My best guess is to ask from genuine curiosity about the person as a person, to better understand who they are...it's happened a handful of times.

## Juan revisited...

Fifteen years later, I reconnected with Juan through social media and he revealed he had liked me back then, but had not known what to do. I collapsed in my mother's kitchen, and then I asked him to dinner that Friday night.

I got up from the kitchen floor and walked to the den in front of my mother's recliner. She had tweezers in one hand and she searched her hairline for grays. I said, "I'm going out with Juan on Friday."

"Juan?" She frowned. "Juan from middle school?"

"Yes."

She leaned into her magnifying mirror. "Oh, cool! When did he ask you out?"

"I asked him. Just now. Oh, God." I sank onto the couch. "I hope he's not another loser. I am so fucking sick of losers."

"*Skittee!* Don't use that word!"

"What? Loser? They are losers. They're beautiful, but they suck. Loser is cheating on someone. Loser is the type who's attracted to me for real. It's like three in a row now. This last one—before he cheated on me with a tall, thin, unexceptional blonde—asked me why he was always attracted to ethnic girls. Like, what the fuck?"

"That's enough about him," she said. "You punched him and that's enough about him."

I talked over her. "Why not ask your fetish why you 'othered' her? And, like, ethnic is a flaw. Every single person has an ethnicity—"

"Oh, shit, Mary Kay, I been it all." She smoothed her hair off her forehead and parted it half an inch farther left. "When I was tending bar, they would say, 'Oh you look like you could be Italian,' and I would say, 'That's 'cause I am!'"

I thought to myself, *That was when all that Qaddafi shit was going on, and I didn't want people to think I was from there. Or that I liked women.*

"Mama, none of those things are the same."

"I know. But it was a bar. You say, Lebanese, they say, lesbian?! I din' give a shit what they thought. Ignorant asses," my mama replied.

On our first date, Juan asked about my mother's ethnicity and whether I spoke Arabic. "Only bad words," I said.

He laughed and then asked about my dad. "What does he do for a living nowadays?"

I asked what his parents did. His mother was in the U.S. Army. I asked about his citizenship. He said he was a full citizen, even though he was born in Panama and still kind of considered it his home. I said, "Cool, what does your dad do?"

He told me later, weeks after we labeled our relationship, that of course people at his work applauded his "Mexican" work ethic and asked him how things were done in "Me-hee-co," but the stereotyping did not bother him anymore.

When I flew out of town for a teaching job, I sent him a selfie from the screening line with the caption, "About to be randomly selected!"

I try to take my mother's advice, to not bother with the people who don't matter, but it's hard not to care when I do care. It's equally easy not to care when I don't. I can only care what people think of me when I already respect them. That quality is one that I learned as I grew up and am still practicing, improving.

When I was eighteen, a boy I was in love with told me he never liked traditionally pretty girls. He dated me for a year. Because I was so impressionable, it took months to rebuild my self-image.

In a morning-after game when I was twenty, I told a guy I could tell he was attracted to me by the way he looked at me when I first met him. He said, "I think I was just trying to figure out what you were."

Walking to my friend's house one day when I was twenty-two, an old man on a bicycle cut in front of me and said, "From the back, I thought you was my girlfriend, but now I see you White." I laughed, stunned, not knowing at which part to be offended.

On the Halloween after I turned twenty-four, I wore my mermaid costume. An acquaintance asked if I was dressed as Jasmine from *Aladdin*. I stared at him and said, "I have a fin," and.my friend tells me that was the exactly right response.

Sometimes I yell at my boyfriend Juan when he misspeaks, or when we fight about regular non-race-related problems, or he hurts my feelings. I try not to explode, but I'm sensitive, obviously.

He apologizes for misspeaking.

I apologize for my short fuse and for yelling.

He accepts my apology and then, because he knows my past, and he knows I hate it, he grins and blames my temper on my Arab and Irish heritage.

I scowl to avoid smiling. I say, "Motherfucker, that's racist. You can't talk to me like that just because we're in love."

"Oh, I'm so sorry."

I accept his apology: "You probably misspoke because English is your second language."

He says, "Oh, I'm racist?"

And this is how it goes, the tug of war, because we are kindred souls from more than one corner of the world apiece, and the same shit over and over either wears you down or makes you laugh, and sometimes we get to choose which reaction to have.

Mary Kay McBrayer is Lebanese, Hispanic, Scottish, Irish and Native American. She studied English Literature at the University of West Georgia and holds an MFA in creative writing. Mary Kay has also served through AmeriCorps at a residential treatment facility for at-risk youth.

# JUST A TYPICAL TEENAGER

Jenny Putri Ellis—Bali

*English and Indonesian*

I'm nearly thirteen and just a typical teenager, really. When I'm not in school, I like to go to the mall to spend my pocket money (which I get for washing and feeding our two dogs). I love to catch a movie with my friends, or I'll stay at home and watch movies on my own—I like horror and comedies a lot. We get the Star World television network and I mainly watch Nickelodeon, Disney or the Sky movie channels. I see all the American sitcoms like *The Simpsons,* but my favourite shows are *Sam & Cat* and *Victorious* on Nickelodeon—I *love* the singer and actress, Ariana Grande. If my life was made into a movie, I'd like her to play me!

At school, I like social studies, which is basically geography and history. I'm quite artistic. In our classes we learn about other artists, and we do paintings and drawings ourselves. I like drawing and designing clothes, although I usually draw people in the clothes rather than just a pattern. I want to be a famous fashion designer and own a shop selling my own brand; I want to be as big as Nike or Adidas. I want to be famous.

My name, btw, is Jennifer Putri Ellis. Putri means "princess" or "daughter of," so I'm Princess Jenny or Jenny, Daughter of Ellis. ☺ My friends call me Jenny, or Jenot—my brother in Surabaya named me that, I don't know why. He thought it was kind of funny, and it stuck.

I live near Kuta in Bali, Indonesia—it's very hot here and there are a lot of tourists. I am half English, half Indonesian, and I have an older brother, Kaito, who is half English and half Japanese from Daddy's first partner, but he lives in Australia now. Mummy is from Surabaya, on the main island of Java, and I have a big family over there: grandparents, brothers and sisters from Mummy's first marriage, cousins and nieces. We probably see them about twice a year. I think my Indonesian cousins are very different from me: they're darker skinned, louder and more straightforward. I also have three South African and two English cousins. They are much more like me, except they are very fair, and we only see them every couple of years.

I grew up speaking Indonesian and, up until the age of two or three, that was all I could speak. Daddy always jokes that when we first went to England to see Granny, she got so mad at me because I was just babbling on in Indonesian. "Speak English," she used to say. "I can't understand you!" Daddy taught me a few words, but I started to learn English properly when I went to the International School. Now it's my main language. Sometimes I speak Indonesian with Mummy, but mostly we talk in English. I only speak to Daddy in English; I hate it when he speaks Indonesian, because he's so bad at it!

I speak Javanese with my family in Surabaya, which is their local dialect, but Indonesian is the common language that everybody speaks here. I used to learn Mandarin at my school, but I just gave up on that because it was very hard. So I can speak Javanese, Indonesian and English. But I mainly talk, think and dream in English; I can't imagine dreaming in another language.

There are twenty people in my class at school; most of the children are from China, however, there are a few Australians and some Dutch people from Holland too. They all live in Bali and English is the main language (except in our Indonesian class, when we can only speak Indonesian). I don't see them as any different from me: we all watch the same TV programmes, listen to the same music and share the same culture, so there's no real difference no matter where you're from or what you look like.

My school is actually an Indonesian Catholic School, and my principal is very religious. We have prayers and worship every morning, but there are different classes for each religion. So if you're Muslim, you go to the Muslim class; if you're Christian, you go to the Christian class. I go to the Christian class, and we sing songs and learn stories about Jesus. Daddy and Mummy are both Christians. The rest of the family in Surabaya are Muslim, but Mummy decided at a young age that she wanted to be Christian. It was quite unusual, but the family said that was okay. We're not especially religious, but we are all vaguely Christian and I like to celebrate Christmas!

Living in Bali, sometimes I go to the beach. I like boogie boarding or just paddling around in the sea, but having the beach on your doorstep can get a bit boring. Plus, there is a lot of rubbish on the beach, plastic bags and stuff, so it's not very nice. The main Kuta beach is pretty touristy and trashy. You can find nice beaches further afield, but that takes time, and I have to get Daddy to drive me there.

I can't travel by myself, so I can only travel if Daddy takes me. We go to Surabaya to see my family a couple of times a year. And we went to Europe to see my other cousins. If I could travel more, I would love to do that. I would like to go to America, Australia or Singapore. I don't know anything about America, other than that I want to go there. Maybe New York or Hollywood. I think a lot of celebrities live there and I would like to meet them. I would also like to travel to Australia; Kaito doesn't tell me what it's like there, he doesn't really talk to me. Typical older brother I guess.

Kaito is different to me. He's half Japanese, but doesn't act like it—he doesn't talk about Japan or anything. He doesn't see himself as Japanese. I don't see myself as Indonesian. I think we both see ourselves as English, or maybe American. Kaito is probably more English because he likes football. I really connect with Americans though, because that's what I see on TV. I don't see colour, I just see what people are like. I don't honestly know what nationality I am. Ever since I was little, I have been in an English school and I speak English, so I think I must be English.

If I had one wish, it would be that I would grow up successful and happy.

Jenny Ellis is a thirteen-year-old girl living in Bali, Indonesia with her mum and dad. She is half English, half Indonesian and has a half-English, half-Japanese older brother.

# TWO PASSPORTS, TWO RACES, ONE IDENTITY

Kasama Yotin—Thailand

*Thai and Belgian*

The twenty-first century: the age where technology, telecommunication and medicine have created memorable innovations. An age where intercultural, multicultural and global have become key words describing the society we are living in today. Since the beginning of civilization, different races intermingled through trade, labor migration, military conquest or diplomatic reason. It's my understanding that interracial marriage was largely condemned prior to the nineteenth century where the product of an interracial marriage was seen as impure. Nonetheless, through many struggles, interracial marriage is not seen as a taboo subject in this modern day. It cannot be denied that the numbers of Biracial offspring are surging in the twenty-first century. It is not uncommon to walk down the street and bump into one.

I am a product of an interracial marriage myself, one between the east and the west. My mother is from Thailand (Southeast Asia) and my father is from Belgium (Western Europe). My grandfather objected to the marriage at first because marrying a man from a different race was inappropriate in his eyes.

When asked why it was inappropriate, my grandfather would say, "Because your partner is different." As time passed, my grandfather was able to set aside the differences in physical appearance and culture, and instead looked at my father as a person. Eventually he gave his approval.

I was born in 1985. Much of my childhood was spent in Thailand, with only three years in Belgium when I was in middle school. Due to my father's job, our family had to move to Vietnam for nearly eight years. Every school break I would spend half of my holiday in Thailand and the other half in Europe. I do not resemble my father at all. Every time I walked alongside him, people would stare at us with a quizzical look. I didn't feel comfortable being seen with my father alone in public when I was younger due to all the stares people gave us. People would ask questions about my family and I felt like my privacy was being invaded. I despised myself for not looking like my father in the least. I often thought that things would be much easier if I bore some resemblance to him. As I grew older, the questioning stares became normal and easy to ignore when with my father in public. Sometimes I even used it to my advantage to start up a conversation.

Even though I hold two passports, there is no need to be left confused with my appearance, because I look fully Asian. People normally judge others by their appearances; I don't blame them because that's the first thing we notice. Nevertheless, in my case, looking like one doesn't mean I possess the same mind-set as one. Because I look Asian, people expect me to follow the cultural norm of Asian tradition. They are in for a surprise and left wondering why I don't think or act like other Asians do.

I have to admit that when I was young, my cultural identity confused me. I didn't feel I fit anywhere, whether in Thailand or Belgium. I was raised in an international environment, I went to international schools since I was young and my parents weren't very traditional. When I spent time with my Thai family, I often got scolded for not acting like the traditional Thai lady. My Thai family expected me to not talk back to them, to be obedient toward elders and to know all of the Thai manners since my mother is Thai.

This is where the confusion started, because Westerners value certain qualities that the Thais see as unbecoming. For example, asking questions is a sign of participating and being open minded in a Western culture, but in a Thai society, questioning elders is looked down upon. I didn't understand why I would get in trouble if I questioned my Thai teachers or my Thai family members since my father encouraged me to analyze and question things. If I was in Thailand, friends and family saw me as being bold, overly confident and liberal, whereas the opposite happened when I went back to Belgium. In Belgium, people viewed me as being shy, not very talkative and not a confident girl. I lived within two cultures, switching back and forth, but through time, I've learned what is to be expected in each culture and I adapt myself according to the culture I'm living in, yet remain as an individual. I can see my little sister going through the same cycle as I did. She lives in Jerusalem with my parents at this moment, and she often complains about cultural expectation crises she faces when spending holidays in Thailand. Hopefully, through time, she will learn to be an individual who can integrate with many cultures.

In addition to the "cultural identity crisis," which I have mentioned above, there is yet another decision to make when you are a by-product of interracial marriage: to which country do you hold your loyalty? To which country should you feel more attached? Do you want to start a family in your mother's home country or your father's home country? I have chosen mine, even though my father still can't decide where he wants to retire. My mother has voiced her strong decision already that she wishes to end up living in Thailand. It would be very sad if my father chooses to retire in Belgium. It is natural to want to live in one's own motherland when one is growing old. I understand both of my parents, but if they both do what their hearts desire, then I cannot visit both of them at the same time.

Though I've experienced cultural identity crises, there are benefits in being a multicultural citizen as well. The most obvious benefit is possessing more than one language. Being able to speak more than one language has opened many doors and horizons to me; the opportunity in finding more jobs, the chance to travel and the many different groups of people I meet. The second benefit is the exposure of many cultures has shaped me into an open-minded person. I am willing to work with people from different racial backgrounds. It makes me understand not to put people into stereotypes just because of what they look like. This is beneficial in the workplace, since the world has become globally connected. People of different continents have to integrate in a workplace. This makes the working experience in an international environment flow smoothly without conflict.

Now at the age of twenty-nine, living in the United States and six months pregnant, I cannot help but wonder what my son will face once he is born. He will hold three passports: American, Belgian and Thai. Will he be able to experience the best of all worlds and adapt, no matter which cultural setting he's put into? Will he attach himself to one country and not the other? There is no definite answer and only through time will all be revealed.

Kasama Yotin is half Thai and half Belgian. She holds a Bachelor's Degree in English Communication and teaches English to ESL (English as a second language) students. She frequently works as a translator.

# THE PROCESS OF KILLING PRECONCEIVED IDEAS ABOUT WHO WE ARE

Maja Dezulovic—South Africa

*Black South African and Croatian*

I was born in Johannesburg, South Africa in 1988. My mother is a Tswana woman and my father is a Croatian immigrant who came to South Africa in the 1960s. At the time, my parents were not legally allowed to have a relationship, never mind get married and have children. Although I cannot really say I experienced Apartheid, being born at the fringe of the New Constitutional Era in South Africa meant that the after-effects were a part of my daily personal life. Dealing with the fact that I was different from most kids was a defining part of my journey into adulthood.

The process of letting go of preconceived ideas about what we think we are supposed to be can be likened to the one we go through when we experience loss, but the outcome goes beyond mere acceptance and progresses to enlightenment, reached by embracing who we are and letting it empower us.

## Denial

When I was young, my mother and I spent a lot of time in the township where she grew up. Although Apartheid was slowly coming to an end and some of its ridiculous laws were no longer being enforced, it was still illegal for a non-White person to live in a White suburb like where my father stayed. I remember how it felt to stick out among the crowd in the townships. When I was a baby, I looked pale with black curly hair—I resembled a young Eastern European child rather than a mixed-race baby. Because of this, my mother was once accused of "stealing a White baby" whilst commuting with me in a minibus taxi, and when we'd arrive in the townships, other kids would point at me and shout, "Look, it's a White kid!" In those days there were not many pale-skinned faces in the townships, and I couldn't help but feel frightened and cling to my mother when the stares and the shouting began.

I felt out of place in the outside world, but I was always safe at home where my mother's family treated me like the other children and showered me with love. At home I was in denial that there were any differences between me and anybody else.

## Anger

Anger set in as I spent more and more time outside of home. When I started school, I was one of the few non-White pupils in the class. Racism was not a problem; I felt no animosity from any adults or any of the children as a result of race, but it was the mere fact that I looked different that caused me to feel ashamed. The black curls gradually grew into an orange afro and I developed freckles on my face, a gift from my red-headed ancestors on my father's side. This gave me the appearance resembling that of a clown and I was therefore an easy target for teasing. As a result, I often ended up in fights with other children and I hated the way I looked.

Later on in life, my anger became more directed towards the ignorance and prejudice of people who chose to judge me based on the way I looked.

## Bargaining

There were times during my childhood when I'd go to bed hoping that I'd wake up in the morning to realise that my life up until that point had only been a dream. Thanks to daytime soap operas and films I'd watched, I fantasized about being in a coma and waking up to the discovery that everything in my life was actually perfect. I even prayed. Like many kids do, I told God that if he gave me a break, I'd focus more on being a better person.

## Depression

Most, if not all, teenagers suffer from some form of depression. At this stage in our lives, we try to figure out who we are and where we want to be. This was not easy for me. In order to figure myself out, I had to rediscover my childhood and look at it from a new angle. This meant moving overseas, away from my family and examining the situation from outside the box.

I went to counselling with a psychologist, and I was taking increasing amounts of antidepressants until I decided that this was not the route I wanted to take. I chose to be alone, far from home, so that I could evaluate the situation without being in it. Luckily, my family and friends were understanding and their love and support helped me progress.

This experience was life-changing.

## Acceptance

Although I was the only person of colour in my school for a long time, studying at an international school in Zagreb, Croatia exposed me to a mix of different people from around the world. In our school environment, we were all unique in some way. There were no preconceived prejudices, and we grew to know each other based on personality and merit.

Over time, I stopped being emotional about people's ignorance. That would help me again later in my life when I met my White husband, who came from a strict Afrikaans-speaking background with friends and family who were not initially open-minded about associating themselves with a "coloured woman."

I emerged out of this phase able to look myself in the mirror and truly think that I was beautiful. It was also the time of a rising trend in social media, so posing for countless selfies also helped. I began to accept all the things that made up the whole me.

Being in a different environment and having the opportunity to explore parts of Europe also inspired my love of travelling and helped pull me through the depression phase.

## Embracing

After accepting who and what I was, I began to realise how valuable and fun it could be to be me. I interacted with many different cultures and I realised that rather than not fitting into any social or cultural group, I could fit into any of them with ease because I could adapt based on my knowledge and experiences.

Before that I hadn't looked at my life as special, but the more I embraced it, the more I gained pride in the little details of it. One such example was our daily life at home. Dinner guests often remarked that they seldom heard so many languages at one table: my sister and I spoke to each other in English, we spoke to our father in Croatian and my mother communicated in Tswana. Additionally, my parents conversed in Zulu. Afrikaans, a form of Old Dutch spoken in South Africa, was a language we were introduced to when we began our schooling and it was added to the table when I met my husband. I often smile when I look at how diverse we are in these ordinary situations.

## Empowerment

I realised that my mixed background had allowed me to experience several different cultures that made up a part of who I was. When I learned that these traits were not common, I allowed them to become a part of the definition of my own identity. How many people can say that they can speak five languages? I can, and there are many other experiences resulting from my background that have added knowledge and skills for which I am grateful.

I believe that being multiracial is an advantage. We are the evolution of the human race and we exist beyond racism and social niches. Throughout history, many wars and struggles happened as a result of people valuing one race, religion or culture over others, and although in many places this form of judgement is still commonplace, humanity is progressing beyond it. People like me are proof of this and that the face of the world is changing. In fact, the "mixed race" is the fastest growing race in America and perhaps even the world. By mid-century, we will be the dominant race in North America.

The beauty of it is that the mixed race is not defined by any single culture, religion or creed. We also easily adapt to new situations and we are statistically healthier than our "pure bred" counterparts, which are essential evolutionary traits. We represent the mixing of cultures and ideas, and the exposure of the individualities that we sometimes fail to recognise as a result of focusing on similarities. There are many similarities between people. It is our differences that make us unique. So embrace your uniqueness and let it empower you.

Maja Dezulovic is a South African/Croatian writer. She spent her childhood in South Africa and her late teenage years in Croatia, and then hopped between Africa and Europe until finally deciding to settle in Croatia. Her lifestyle has allowed her to gain varied insights into different people and places. As a result, she has many interests that emerge in her work.

Maja works full time as a ghostwriter, article writer and blogger. She has published two poetry anthologies (*The 360 Degree Heart* and *Expressions of Humanity*—both of which are available on Amazon), and is working on a dystopian fiction novel. When she's not writing, she keeps herself busy by coordinating an art route through an old town called Janjina. Maja lives by the beautiful Adriatic Sea in a nineteenth-century villa with her husband Luke and Leeto the cocker spaniel.

Maja's website: http://bluedaisiesandpurplegrass.blogspot.co.uk

# BIRACIAL BY ASSOCIATION

Bridget Ivins-Young—United States

*White, Mother of a Black and White Child*

My very closest loved ones are Biracial, Black and White: specifically, my only sister, a brother, my husband and my son. My son is one-quarter Black, but he definitely looks Black. When I say Black, I know he is mixed with my European heritage, Irish and Welsh, mostly. But what my husband impressed upon me early in our relationship is that in the U.S., if you look even a little Black, you are Black.

My husband has many stories, though, of how in social situations among other Black kids, he was not Black enough for them. Incidentally, his mother was first generation German, coming here at the end of WWII as a refugee. Her family landed in the Bronx (one of the five boroughs of New York City), and she had her first mixed-race child (my husband's only sister) in the mid 1950s when she was fifteen years old.

I was so delighted at twelve to get a sister (I had one brother at this point and we were far from close), but my mother kept reminding me she would be mixed, as if I would have a problem with it. I think she may have had a problem somehow.

My sister and I were very close; at home she was my world until I left to live with my grandmother at the age of sixteen. My mother never really encouraged my sister to embrace her Black heritage or culture. When she came to visit me in California, she and my husband had a few heart-to-heart talks about being mixed. I remember my husband feeling it important to impress upon her that she was Black. She kept saying how she was Irish too. He kept telling her how she needed to "get" that she was Black. My sister now lives in Florida where she has faced some pronounced racism in many forms, including coworkers thinking it was funny to cover her car in watermelon after Barack Obama won his second term as President of the United States.

I would like to meet these assholes.

My husband has a family like mine. He is Biracial and has some siblings who are not—two White brothers whom he grew up with in the same household, as well as some all Black siblings from his father's first marriage.

Rudy, one of his White brothers, didn't seem to care he had mixed siblings, but the other one tried to disassociate himself from them in social situations as a child, including asking Rudy to not let other campers at sleep-away camp know that "those kids" (my husband and his twin brother) were their brothers.

My husband never discussed how this made him feel, but this is not my favorite brother-in-law. Incidentally, Rudy proceeded to let the whole camp know who his brothers were. Bravo, Rudy!

I have had, over most of my adult life, a more intimate view of what it's like to be Black and Biracial in America than I'd say most White Americans. I don't know what it is to be Biracial, but I do know what it is to be a minority. I worked in heavy construction for the local gas company where my coworkers were 99 percent men. I was a minority as a woman, but the racism was what was very unsettling. It was so entrenched and unconscious. A good ol' boys network was firmly in place.

There were jokes made about the old days, when a foreman hid a snake in the Black guy's lunchbox and "you know how Blacks are scared of snakes, hardy harhar." A guy once said he didn't believe in mixed marriages (like they are the tooth fairy?) because, what about the kids? Or comments about a basketball players' names, how "they" sure give their kids weird names.

When I had been around long enough, someone discovered my husband's ethnicity. My foreman actually approached me and said that he'd heard my husband was Black, and he wanted to know if this was true. When I told him yes, and that specifically he was Black and German (this foreman happened to be German, a former lumberjack from Oregon, dumber than a box of rocks) he said to me, and I kid you not, "How can that be?"

There were a couple of days when I came home (my husband chuckled at this, but it is truly how I felt), that I wanted to go hang out with our Black friends. I have tried to get why I felt this urge and have come up with I think I needed to feel like I was with someone I could trust.

I have lived most of my life in the San Francisco Bay Area of California. I can say that having lived in New York City and having traveled a bit to other states, I am lucky to live in a very culturally diverse community with a very large Biracial and multiracial community.

I love it here. My son is Biracial and I would say that in his school of 700+ kids, probably one in fifteen or twenty are also Biracial or multiracial. I love this too.

This past weekend, I took my son to a favorite park and there were about six or seven kids there. One was a group of White kids and another a group of Black kids, all around his age. They were playing separately and David played with one group, then the other, and then back again—like a kind of little unconscious emissary.

I recounted our time in the park to my husband, and he told me how at times he had different groups of friends when he was a kid. Groups of White friends and groups of Black friends. He was part of both "cliques," but they didn't mingle with each other.

I love that our president is Biracial (it helps that I like most of what he's accomplished as well) and that my son is a child in some very formative and impressionable years during Obama's presidency.

A few years ago my husband and I were watching an episode of *Heroes*. There were several storylines, one of which involved a couple and their child and how they were dealing with their newly-discovered superpowers. The mom on the show was White and the dad was Black. I commented to my husband how if it were ten or fifteen years ago, that is what the show would have been about—race.

Although I am not Biracial, I am surrounded by multiracial people and so I feel as though I am "Biracial by association," and it's a group I am proud to belong to.

Bridget and her husband, Sterling, both grew up in New York City, where they met as teenagers. They have been together for over thirty years. They both come from very diverse backgrounds: Bridget is White and she has both White and Biracial siblings, while Sterling is Biracial and has Biracial, Black and White siblings.

Bridget and her husband live in the San Francisco Bay area. They have one son named David.

# NIGGER NIGGER PULL THE TRIGGER: ONE MORE VIEW FROM THE PERIPHERY OF THE MASTER RACE

Mark White—Australia

*Barbadian and White*

My name is Mark. I have Alumni Association prize-winning university degrees in Archaeology and Anthropology and a postgraduate diploma in Dance. I have spoken, performed and choreographed for hundreds of thousands of people in cities all over the world. I have worked on Academy Award-winning films; made award-winning dance, film and other projects of my own. There's even a gold medal in sport amongst too many accolades to comfortably mention here.

I am as at ease in front of forty thousand as I am in front of four and seldom find myself searching for words. And yet I've struggled to write this piece. Simply because I am conflicted in my judgement: just as mixed as the blood running through my veins. All of the above opportunity I owe in principle to the circumstances of my upbringing. And yet I have judged those who reared me and found them to be grievously wanting.

I was adopted by a White couple who brought me out of the tiny island of Barbados and the massive implications of its rigid Black-to-White pyramid hierarchy. They moved to the White middle-class West and gave me a White middle-class education in White middle-class neighbourhoods that afforded me the opportunities above and so much more: opportunities otherwise impossible for a coloured child in the 1960s, 1970s and 1980s when I grew up.

Much has changed since then. Much has not. I am intensely aware of, and deeply grateful for, the rich and rewarding tapestry of my life. But I am also deeply saddened by the loss of my birthright. For all the opportunity my adopted parents provided, they also robbed me of vital opportunities. The opportunity to be coloured. The opportunity to belong.

Instead of this, I was different as a child. A thing to be poked and teased.

A thing that did not fit in, was not allowed in. And as I grew older, I became more than just different to the White middle class I had grown up within, been dressed like, forced to live in and doggedly taught to think like. I became what they could see of me. I became Black. Not coloured. Not mixed. Not Mark. Just Black.

I have thought long and hard about what I might be able to contribute to a conversation such as this book you are reading. It is only the one idea.

*Race is not a level playing field. A child of mixed race is a thing of the future and not one of the present. Until such time as race does not matter, those who are responsible for raising mixed children must balance their cultural education and protection so that they are afforded the same sense of identity and belonging AND the same opportunities as those of the dominant culture. No easy task, but if you can't take the heat, I suggest you go cook in your own kitchen.*

To my mind it does not matter how you came to be responsible for a child of mixed race. Only that you have in your care a growing person from two worlds who has the right to feel equally comfortable in either. If you cannot provide that, then you will harm the child and you will be guilty of abuse.

I have spent my life profoundly affected by the fact that the regulatory environment surrounding the ownership of a dog is superior to that of childrearing, which, while subjected to the dominant cultural architecture externally, lacks the guaranteed protection of responsible parenting in the home.

If this piece is inflammatory, if I seem ungrateful and judgemental, then I will have achieved my goal. Coupling with someone outside your racial position is your business. Producing mixed offspring is another matter altogether. At that point, all that matters are the many issues that confront children of mixed blood.

How will your children be treated outside the home? Where will they live? Where will they go to school? How will

your extended families treat an addition that is neither one thing nor the other? What language will you speak in the home? How will you protect your children and provide them with an environment that fosters a secure sense of place? If you do not have the answers to these questions and many more, you are unfit to parent children of mixed race.

So that is all that I have to offer up to the conversation around the issues of being mixed race. I could speak here about listening to "Uncles" and "Aunts" laugh and joke about the "niggers back at home" or of my childhood antics being "the nigger coming out in him." I could speak of lacking positive role models, of being viewed and treated as other in the home, as inferior in the home. I could speak of a childhood of terror: of physical, racial, mental and sexual abuse from either the nuclear or extended "family." I could speak of so much teasing and torture and discrimination and self-hatred, and so very much more.

But in the end, I would only be repeating my core contribution to this discussion. So I will close with that simple paragraph and hope that I have moved someone to think about the ramifications of mixed race in a world that is becoming less culturally tolerant even as it becomes more racially mixed.

*Race is not a level playing field. A child of mixed race is a thing of the future and not one of the present. Until such time as race does not matter, those who are responsible for raising mixed children must balance their cultural education and protection so that they are afforded the same sense of identity and belonging AND the same opportunities as those of the dominant culture. No easy task, but if you can't take the heat, I suggest you go cook in your own kitchen.*

*I wish your children well.*

Mark was born in Barbados to a Black father and White teenage unwed mother. He has never been able to discover anything else about his parents, as he was adopted not long after birth by a White family who emigrated with him to New Zealand.

A graduate of the Royal New Zealand School of Dance in the late 1980s, Mark toured the world as a dancer with Limbs Dance Company before forming his own two-year project, Full of Piranhas Dance Company. The innovative dance project toured and performed extensively through New Zealand and the Pacific, including a number of Command Performances for various members of the Royal Family. While touring Australia in the stage show *Ladies' Night,* Mark decided to make the move to Sydney where he was a frequent performer and producer of shows for the commercial and club scenes. Probably most noticed amongst his work is *The Adventures of Priscilla, Queen of the Desert,* for which he was engaged as choreographer and physical coach. A prolific artist, Mark also produced and starred in *The Caretaker,* and recently starred in two short films that will be submitted to Tropfest this year.

The Caretaker: http://www.thecaretakerfilm.com

# MIXED UP?

Bryony Sutherland—England, United Kingdom

*White; Mother of three Caribbean Black and White children*

## Being In Love

I was fifteen when I met my partner. He was two years older, had just the right blend of humour, confidence and charisma, and was handsome enough to capture my teenage heart. We flirted shamelessly on our shared school bus for a year while we got exams out of the way—A-levels for him, GCSEs for me—then, just as I was sure I'd never see him again, he asked me out. My girlish angst—did he really like me, or was he just playing with me—dissipated and I embarked on my first serious romantic relationship. A quarter of a century later and we're still together, still in love, married now with three sons. A happy life.

Did I ever think about the colour of his skin? Truly, no. When I saw him, my young heart fluttered at his big brown eyes, his easy smile and the way he somehow made me feel special, different to the other girls demanding his attention. He was the only Black guy at his school—otherwise packed with Whites and Asians—but it didn't faze him. He was popular, intelligent, self-assured, and seemed to have a bright future ahead. So why should the fact that he was Black and I was White faze me?

When it became clear that this wasn't a passing teenage crush, my parents welcomed him into our family. Well, with my mother's unique sense of humour, that actually entailed chasing him round the kitchen with a bread knife if he dared to contradict her, but that was the test. Could he take her on and laugh with her? Even come back for more? He could. He continues to, to this day. The parental seal of approval.

Which was just as well really, because family circumstances dictated that I move in with my boyfriend while I was still at school. Two years later, when it was my turn to take A-levels, my beloved grandmother's allotted few weeks to live stretched into many long months. Saying goodbye multiple times was hard on my little family (I have no siblings), so my parents agreed it was better for my exam prospects if I stayed with a friend for a while. A pupil living with her boyfriend was unheard of at my single-sex school, but we got away with it. And when my parents called to tell me my grandmother had passed away on the day of my English exam (they waited till the next day to tell me), I cried in my boyfriend's arms, with his mother sitting right next to me, her hand on my knee.

My parents brought me up in a liberal manner. They knew that if they pushed me too hard in one direction I would rebel. It was a brave decision, with a single daughter as their only offspring, but it worked. Although I never returned home, my relationship with my parents remains incredibly strong, largely due to the freedom they allowed me to forge my own life. My boyfriend and I moved to London that summer, earning the rent on a series of crumbling studio flats with a series of dreadful jobs, and there we stayed, through two degrees, marriage and, ultimately, children.

## Being Interracial

It's not hard to be a mixed-race couple in London. I should specify as my aim with this essay is not to generalise but to report solely on my experience: it's not hard to be a mixed-race couple in North and Central London, where we lived for twelve years. London is a melting pot and our friends came from all walks of life. Their complexions were wide and varied, and no one ever hesitated if a romantic partner had a different heritage. Our friends were predominantly involved in the music, sports and film industries, all of which harboured a healthy attitude towards equality and racial harmony in this country. We were by no means the only mixed couple, particularly within the sporting social circles, and to be frank, we were probably even a little conservative for some of our more colourful friends. So you're mixed? So what? Move on.

No one ever, ever made a big deal—or any sized deal—out of our mixed cultures. Once only did we provoke a reaction. About twenty years ago, we were walking hand-in-hand down the high street in Wood Green, and two Black girls were walking in the opposite direction. As they passed us, they shot a look of disgust at my partner and one of them spat at my feet. A

fleeting moment I'll never forget. The main reason it's etched in my memory being the fact it was an isolated incident.

My attitude towards race is also shaped by my husband's experiences. I've seen him grow from a determined seventeen-year-old boy to a successful businessman in his forties, and I can honestly say that the colour of his skin has never held him back. Nor has he ever found himself in a position where it might hold him back, especially in terms of his career. In fact, it probably works to his advantage. In London at least, the major companies need to be seen as promoting equal opportunities. It reflects well on them to have a Black man in a senior position. And once you're in that senior position, well, only a fool would dare be racist to you. So is that "playing the race card?" I don't know. My husband works hard and brings enthusiasm and experience to any job. Any company is lucky to have him. The money he earns in return puts food on the table and a roof above our heads.

In the UK, inherent racial discrimination can be narrowed down to different parts of the country, predominantly cities. For example, my husband grew up in an area where crime rates were high. Stop and Search was very much in place during his teenage years. Twice the police stopped him—once when he was walking home with a White friend, once when he was alone—and questioned him as to his evening's whereabouts. It went no further, because in both cases he was demonstrably not part of any criminal activity, but it's not an experience one forgets in a hurry.

Asking him recently when he'd last experienced racism of any kind, he frowned, so I changed the question. How many times a day? A week? A month? His answer was...maybe once every two months. What kind? Perhaps standing at a bar and not being served first. (This, of course, is not necessarily quantifiable by race. It takes me ages to get served. I'm female, I'm short and I don't shout as loud as the others.)

I then asked him if he'd ever experienced racism as a by-product of going out with me. He said once some guys asked him what was wrong with mixing with his own kind. Once. And in the research for this essay, I also discovered his estranged father's reaction to the first time he brought me home was to ask why he was wasting his time on a White girl. But apparently that was just a typical racist statement for him. And it happened just the once.

## Being Biracial

Of course, it doesn't matter a jot what your own experiences are when it comes to having kids. They're not living life in a mixed-race couple; they are that mixed race. And by default, that means distinct differences in their looks, in others' attitudes towards them, and in their perception of their place in the world.

We always knew that we wanted children and fantasised from quite early in our relationship as to what they might look like. We'd seek Biracial people out in public, privately admiring the way features blended between the two races: the curls, the honeyed skin tone, the anomalies in eye colour. I know I lay myself bare for criticism here for a gross sweeping statement, but in a mixed-up world where Black people chemically straighten their hair and White people slather on the fake tan or bake themselves in the name of beauty, Biracial people have a distinct advantage.

I tested myself occasionally during my first pregnancy. When the baby arrived, would he look enough like me for him to feel mine? How would others perceive us? I knew, deep down, that it would be a different life for us as mother and son if he turned out to be very much darker, or inherited none of my features. In the event, when this amazing greyish-pink creature lay on my belly for the first time, any concerns flew out the window. He was a true mixture between the love of my life and me, and that was enough. For three years we continued living in London. I never felt anything less than accepted. Not on the street, not at the shops, not in the park, not out with our friends. My boy was never the "only one" at preschool or playgroups. Mixing cultures is the norm in London. In fact, when I returned to work part time, a close friend became his childminder, bringing him up with her own twin daughters who were a heart-stoppingly beautiful blend of Japanese and Argentinian.

Twelve years later and one has become three. My sons share a strong family resemblance. They form a tribe of their own. Their curls range from dark brown to blond highlights in the summer time, their skin is a glorious caramel and their eyes span hazel to my husband's deep chocolate.
A genetic hand-me-down from my side of the family meant that all three suffered complications with feeding as newborns, and two of them underwent surgery at the ages of six and four weeks respectively. When you've lived through that as a parent, it's not hard to celebrate the fact my boys are now, quite literally, the picture of health. They're strong, fit and sporty, bursting with energy. They will rule the world.

Yes, of course most people comment they look just like their dad. In fact, when she first met us, a dear White South African friend mistook me for their childminder. Years later we still laugh about this. Does this bother me? Not much. Sensibly I know that boys generally resemble their fathers in as much as girls resemble their mothers, and a mini-me is neither appropriate nor likely in my case. Furthermore, I see my own father in my middle son's cheeky grin. And my youngest son was born with blue eyes that gradually changed to brown but retained a distinct greenish segment. That's me in there.

When our family grew, we purposely moved out of London and into a town where we felt comfortable as a mixed race couple. We took great care over this, week after week driving to different towns and villages, walking around observing the racial mix for ourselves, visiting schools, speaking to friends living in the area. Research when you're uprooting is something most couples undertake unless time is a factor, but for us it has that extra element. Are there other families like us out there? When you look around a crowded bar or restaurant or shopping mall, are people mixing? Again, I

 should specify at this point that we're not just talking Black and White to mirror our own situation; we want our children to grow up surrounded by every culture possible. When we did make the break from the safety of London's melting pot, we knew it was right for us.

Needless to say, over the next ten years we were welcomed into the community. My children attended schools where classmates visibly shared their racial heritage. They felt comfortable. We brought them up to respect all cultures and backgrounds, and it was interesting to watch my eldest form a 'band of brothers' in his last few years at primary school, where his three best friends were White, Black (adopted by a mixed couple—Black and White) and Biracial (Italian White and Caribbean Black). I hasten to add this was no special school, just one typical of the area where we live.

At home we took care to include West Indian as well as English influences. As a writer, books are hugely important to me and I sought out the few bedtime story books pertaining to our family (Floella Benjamin's gorgeous *My Two Grannies* and Marguerite W Davol's *Black, White, Just Right* becoming firm favourites). I bought Black parenting books so as to better understand our responsibilities as parents, yet I found the issues they focused on did not affect my sons. Their grandmother cooks them West Indian food, and we expose them to as much mixed culture in terms of music and entertainment as they can soak up. Admittedly we are not part of a large West Indian community, but we do what we can.

A year ago, when the idea for this book was first conceived, I asked my eldest whether he considered himself to be Biracial, Black or White. He said Biracial. He felt that if he said he was Black, he'd be discounting half of his family. If he said he was White, the same. Why would he do that, he asked, when he could have the best of both worlds? He said once—once—a friend had asked him if he'd prefer to be Black or White. He said neither: he's both.

I then asked him if he felt anyone had ever been racist to him. He asked in return, if someone says you're a really good runner because you're half Black, is that being racist? We smiled. No, we said, it's a compliment. (There's no dark underlying meaning to that comment. In the UK, the percentage of mixed race athletes is striking; likewise singers, musicians and actors. The European and Commonwealth silver medallist sprinter, Jodie Williams, and the singer and TV personality, Alesha Dixon, hail from my home turf, with Formula 1 racing driver Lewis Hamilton coming from a neighbouring town.) Since then, my son's world has expanded as he progresses through the school system, and meeting new people has exposed gaps in others' understanding of certain racial terms. We meet each new challenge with the aim of broadening education and increasing tolerance, and fortunately these instances are few and far between.

I have, of course, heard that some people will always consider a Biracial person to be Black. One White friend (married to a Black woman) told me that he has had to "overcome" the idea that his two kids will be considered by the world at large to be a different colour to him. Have I ever been bothered about this? No. Am I living in a bubble? Yes, according to everything I've learned researching and compiling this book. But I don't consider my boys to be Black. I consider them to be Biracial.

In the UK, where there is no 'one drop' rule, every time we have to fill out an official form there are boxes to tick. They don't just cover Black, White, Asian, etc. No. There's a box for a mixed relationship any which way. It used to be a choice of four: White/Black Caribbean and White/Black African being two of them. Now there are about a dozen boxes to choose from. So in the eyes of the law, the government, their birth certificates, the taxman, their future employers—you name it—my kids are Biracial.

## Being Human

As Sarah says, "We can't unlearn what we know. We can't pretend history didn't happen. We can learn to live in the world we live in, but we can't simply live with blinders on."

In many ways, my racial education began with the creation of this book.

When I bluntly stated I was "colour blind" early on in our creative partnership, was I in fact wearing blinders, or blinkers as they are known in my country? My co-author's experiences were so very different to my own, and it prompted me to learn more about the contrasting levels of acceptance in other countries across the globe. Prior to reading her essay, I never really understood when she told me that she identified Black—to me that meant discounting three quarters of her heritage. Not that I didn't respect her choice before—I did—but now I know her history, and more about how her family's history is entwined with the Black Panthers and the Biafran War (both frightening, faraway prospects to a White British woman of my age), "to not choose Black means I am living with blinders on, and I can't do that," makes a lot more sense.

The difference between us is that, if I have a choice, I want my children to identify as Biracial. I want the world to allow them to do that, and so far this has not been the major issue that it would be if they were being brought up elsewhere.

What I've learned more than anything else is that some countries and cultures are not yet ready to accept what one of our authors privately called my "future family." It is a sad but likely truth that I will avoid traveling in certain countries while my kids are still young. Yes, gradually we will prepare them for the prejudice they will doubtlessly encounter, but we have high hopes that eventually any prejudice will be eclipsed by progression.

Remembering that race relations in my corner of the UK largely do not mirror those in the U.S. and have not done so during my lifetime, my stance is that the past should never be forgotten, we should continually learn from our mistakes and we should respect those whose lives have been irrevocably affected. BUT we need to move forward in harmony and build a new world through reshaping our attitudes and educating our children. As a parent of three Biracial children, I aim to teach them tolerance, humility and, hopefully, the confidence to be whomever they choose to be in this big ol' mixed-up world.

I know that to many my story will sound ridiculously idealistic, and I acknowledge that so far we have been exceptionally lucky, but as I mentioned earlier, I can only comment with authority on what I've experienced personally. And that is, for nearly a quarter of a century I have lived proudly and peacefully with my husband. Our three children are secure in their skins. They know they are loved, they know they are accepted and they know that they are two things, not one.

And that is special and to be celebrated.

# LET'S TALK

It's difficult to summarize everything we have learned, because to do so would entail writing another book. Due to our family circumstances, neither of us is what we would describe as "intolerant," as our choices and our parents' choices dictate that we are, by default, open-minded. On the one hand, the stories our contributors shared have been enlightening and have taught us many things about race, how people see themselves and how others see them. On the other hand, it has confirmed something we already knew, which is that race remains a very complicated topic and one that, although we've done our best to unravel, is not a discussion we can stop having any time soon.

We would like to thank you for reading our book and we hope that, on some level, these glimpses into *Being Biracial* from all corners of the globe inspire you as they have us. These are our secret worlds, and as they collide, new dialogues, alliances and friendships are formed.

In the spring of 2016 we will publish a companion guide that looks at race and being Biracial from a theoretical perspective. Beyond answering the questions: "What is race?" and "What does it mean to be Biracial?", we delve deeper into comparing and contrasting our experiences, how others perceive us and race as a social construct.

Talking is good. If you'd like to join the discussion, please join us online at:

https://www.facebook.com/beingbiracialanthology
https://twitter.com/BeingBiracialSW
http://beingbiracial.com

*Dif-tor heh smusma*...Live long and prosper

We hope you enjoyed *Being Biracial: Where Our Secret Worlds Collide.* Reviews mean a lot to us as they help us to refine our content and spread the word. Please take a moment to share your thoughts by posting a review at Amazon.com, Amazon.co.uk, Barnes & Noble.com or Goodreads.com.

# COVER ARTWORK

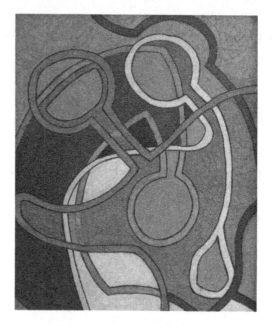

*Blue and Yellow is Always Only Ever About Green*
by Mark White

The male figure is ringed in blue and the yellow ringed female is heavily pregnant; the child in her belly is ringed in green, a blending of blue and yellow. It is the birth of the first and far in the background in brown there is a part of my neck and one ear. Present but forced into the role of observer, as blue and yellow is always only ever about green[19].

---

[19] Mark's essay covers the dual meaning of this picture, as explained in his words above. However, for the purposes of this book, green represents the blending of blue and yellow, making the baby in her belly Biracial.

# ACKNOWLEDGEMENTS

First and foremost, we would like to thank our contributors: without their stories, this book would not exist. When we approached them, a few were friends and many were strangers, but now we count all as friends. So to Souad Aineche, Lea Borinan Bernus, Yacob Cajee, Maja Dezulovic, Sarah Ellingworth, Jenny Putri Ellis, Jamie Dickerson Frayer, Jeremy Gelfand, Erica Hayes, Bridget Ivins-Young, Søren Kaneda, Chance Maree, Mary Kay McBrayer, Sarah Degnan Moje, Amy Myers, Lezel Nel, Janek O'Toole, Heather Rolland, Kim Suree Williamson, Kasama Yotin and those who would prefer to remain anonymous—thank you!

Special mention must go to Mark White, for not only writing a memorable contribution, but also for donating his artwork for the cover. This beautiful picture was sent halfway round the world from Australia to its new home in the UK, where it is already teaching three Biracial boys to analyse and appreciate art with a new eye.

On the topic of the cover, Stephanie Hurtado should take a bow for turning a very rough scribble into our *Being Biracial* logos, and Lisa Thomson has surely won an award for patience in cover and layout design for bearing with at least a gazillion requests and tweaks. For assistance in the online world, our website(s) would not exist without Spencer Penrod and Gwen Mattson.

# Sarah

I would like to thank the following people, for without whom, I would never have been able to take what has been inside my head for years and put it down on paper.

First and foremost, my husband, Paul: He is my rock and my biggest supporter. He sees life through similarly colored glasses and so I never have to explain things to him; he just gets it. I love him with every ounce of my being, and can't thank him enough for his unwavering support, encouragement, suggestions, hugs, patience while Bryony and I worked on the book, doing the laundry and letting me sleep in mornings when I have stayed up late to write.

My parents, George and Emily Orick: Not only did they buck the system and his family, but they never brushed anything under the rug. No subject was taboo in our home growing up and for that I can't thank them enough. There isn't a day that goes by that I don't think about them both and wish they were alive to see the woman I have grown into.

My in-laws: Sylvia Ratliff-Trappio and William and Kathryn Ratliff-Hager have accepted and loved me unconditionally from the first time we met on Thanksgiving Day 1998. Their support and encouragement have meant more to me than I have ever been able to express.

I am eternally grateful to my very first client, Aimee-Jo Davis Varela, who took a chance on this neophyte writer with nothing more than a promise to produce the content she needed.

Everyone who works for me (not specifically mentioned): I own a content marketing agency and during my periods of absence and absent-mindedness as I spent time writing this book and collaborating with Bryony, they have been there to hold me up and cheer me on.

Nathan Falde: History was never a subject I excelled in when I was in school. Nathan (the senior writer on my team) helped me weed through the inordinate amount of information on the Internet so I could include only the most relevant portions for my essay.

My editor, Cathy Habas: Frenetic, an extrovert, dyslexic (Yoda, much?) and prone to going off in tangents (and sometimes forgetting to return) do not a good writer make. Cathy takes what I intended to say and makes sure I actually say it. She's always got my back!

Bryony Sutherland: When I met Bryony in April 2014 I was in awe of her. Co-author or author of ten books and sought-after editor for manuscripts penned by high profile people, I compared my insides to her outsides. As I got to know the person behind the photo and name, I realized how much we have in common and how similarly we see life. When she told me she was married to a Black man and I told her I was Biracial, these were no longer just things that bonded us in friendship but a commonality we both needed to share with others. I am grateful to her for encouraging me to be her co-author. Working with her has been a joy. A true collaborator, there are no egos here: Just two people with a message to deliver. Love and admiration are two words that quickly spring to mind when thinking of Bryony.

## Bryony

My love and gratitude go to my husband, Frankie, for his support and infinite understanding over the last year while Sarah and I collaborated, and to my children, who continue to inspire me with their attitude to life, learning and respect for others. I am so sorry for all the times dinner was late due to Skype calls relating to this book.

Thank you to my parents, Barbara and Peter Newson, for allowing me to follow my heart and supporting my decisions from my teenage years right through to the present day. With you behind me, things worked out pretty well in the end.

A special thanks to my friend and colleague, Lucy Ellis, who not only ghostwrote one of the accounts published in this anthology, but also selflessly helps keep our business afloat, even when times are tough. This means the world to me.

To Tom Conyers, Ian Sutherland and Marilyn Harding, from whom I've learned so much about books and promotion in this strange new publishing age. Each of these authors has also supported this anthology and made introductions for me that changed the course of my career, for which I am forever grateful. Please buy their books—they come highly recommended.

To Peter Gabriel, for writing the music that shaped the lives of two co-authors, and for personally granting Sarah permission to use his 'Secret Worlds' title a lifetime ago. Shh, listen...

And finally to Sarah Ratliff, whose ability to put her experiences aside and take on others' viewpoints continues to surprise and humble me. What people tend not to know about such an outspoken personality are the many small, unspoken kindnesses going on behind the scenes. But I see them, and I know the world is a better place for them. This anthology has transformed us both in so many ways. Sarah, I think it's time to meet in person, don't you?

# BRYONY SUTHERLAND

Bryony Sutherland's writing career began as the co-author of a number of biographies with Lucy Ellis, published by Random House, Virgin Books, Aurum Press, Ebury Press, Omnibus Press, Music Sales, Hannibal, Birmar and Heel Verlag. Together they have been called "professional storytellers" by *The Guardian,* "very professional" by *Film Review,* "immensely readable" by *The Beat Goes On,* "detailed" by *Sunday Express* and "insightful" by *OK! Magazine.* She has written extensively for web and print, for clients ranging from international celebrities to Fortune 100 companies.

Now working as an editor, she specialises in memoirs, lifestyle how-tos and fiction...with a twist. Bryony lives with her husband and three sons in Hertfordshire, England.

For more information, visit http://bryonysutherland.com

# SARAH RATLIFF

F ollowing twenty years in corporate America, in 2008 Sarah and her husband gave up their jobs to relocate from California to Puerto Rico to be self-sustaining organic farmers.  Within a year, it was evident one of them needed to return to work. Dreading the notion of commuting and the office politics so common in the corporate world, Sarah opted to live out her life-long dream of becoming a writer. A week after hanging her "Writer for hire" sign out, Sarah landed multiple jobs. Within three months, she had to hire more writers.

Nearly a decade later, Sarah is the CEO of a content marketing agency. In December 2015 Sarah founded Coquí Press, a publishing company whose mission is to give a voice to those whose views run counter to the mainstream or whose voices have been silenced because of race, gender and/or sexual orientation. In March 2016, along with the host of the

Multiracial Family Man podcast, Alex Barnett, Sarah co-founded Multiracial Media: *Voice of the Multiracial Community,* which is a platform of artistic expression for the Multiracial Community.

For more information, visit: http://coquicontentmarketing.com, http://coquipress.com, http://mayanifarms.com, http://sarahratliff.com, http://multiracialmedia.com.

CPSIA information can be obtained
at www.ICGtesting.com
Printed in the USA
LVOW03s0219131017
552254LV00020B/1175/P